Contents

Introduction to

Madrid

The sunniest, highest and livliest capital city in Europe, Madrid has a lot to take pride in. Indeed, its inhabitants, the Madrileños, are so proud of their city that they modestly declare "desde Madrid al Cielo": that from Madrid there is only one destination left – Heaven. While their claim might be debatable, this compact, frenetic and fascinating city certainly has bags of appeal and its range of attractions is fast making it a deservedly popular short-break destination.

What had previously been a Moorish stronghold and then a small Christian garrison town became Spain's capital in 1561 thanks to the whim of one man, Felipe II. The site possessed few natural advantages – a fierce climate, no harbour and a poor excuse for a river – but it lay exactly in the centre of Spain, and Felipe based the

▼ Madrid nightlife

Madrid

DIRECTIONS

WRITTEN AND RESEARCHED BY

Simon Baskett

**ROUGH
GUIDES**

NEW YORK • LONDON • DELHI
www.roughguides.com

When to visit

Traditionally, Madrid has a typical **continental climate**, cold and dry in winter, and hot and dry in summer. There are usually two rainy periods, in October/November and any time from late March to early May. With temperatures soaring to over 40ºC in July and August, the best times to visit are generally **spring** and **autumn**, when the city is pleasantly warm. The short, sharp winter takes many visitors by surprise, but crisp, sunny days with clear blue skies compensate for the drop in temperature.

Although Madrid is increasingly falling into line with other European capitals, much of it still shuts down in **summer**. For around six weeks from the end of July, many of the inhabitants head for the coast or countryside. Luckily for visitors, and those Madrileños who choose to remain, sights and museums remain open and nightlife takes on a momentum of its own.

formerly itinerant court here to avoid giving too much power to any one region. Following an initial golden age when literature and the arts flourished with the likes of Cervantes and Velázquez, centuries of gradual decline and political turmoil followed, leaving Madrid with a slightly parochial image. Following the death of the dictator Franco in 1975 and the return to democracy, however, the city had a second burst of creativity, *La Movida Madrileña*, an outpouring of hedonistic, highly innovative and creative forces embodied by film director Pedro Almodóvar.

Today Madrid remains a thriving if somewhat chaotic modern capital.

Millions of visitors head straight for the **Prado**, the **Reina Sofía** and the **Thyssen-Bornemisza**, three magnificent galleries that give the city a strong claim to being "European capital of art". Of equal appeal to football fans is one of the world's most glamorous and successful clubs, **Real Madrid**. Aside from these, there's also a host of smaller museums, palaces and parks which, when combined with some of the best **tapas** in Spain, countless bars and legendary nightlife, makes it easy to see why so many people get hooked when they come here.

Madrid's short but eventful history has left behind

▼ Thyssen-Bornemisza gallery .

▲ Plaza de la Cibeles

a mosaic of traditions, **cultures** and **cuisines**, and you soon realize that it is the inhabitants who play a big part in the city's appeal. Hanging out in the cafés or on the summer *terrazas*, packing the lanes of the Rastro flea market, filling the restaurants or playing hard and very, very late in a thousand bars and clubs, Madrileños have an almost insatiable appetite for enjoying themselves. The **nightlife** for which Madrid is renowned is merely an extension of the Madrileño character and the capital's inhabitants consider other European cities positively dull by comparison with their own.

The city centre with its characterful mix of bustling, labyrinthine streets and peaceful squares, punctuated by historic

▼ Tapas

architectural reminders of the past, is in better shape now than for many years thanks to ongoing urban **regeneration** schemes in the older barrios (districts). However, the local council's obsession for grandiose construction projects means that the city appears to be under repair for much of the time. As with many of its international counterparts, an influx of fast-food and coffee chains has challenged the once dominant local bars and restaurants, but, nevertheless, in making the transition from provincial backwater just thirty years ago to major European capital today, Madrid has managed to preserve many key elements of its own stylish and quirky identity.

Madrid
AT A GLANCE

▲ Plaza Santa Ana

MADRID DE LOS AUSTRIAS

Centred around the grandiose Plaza Mayor, Madrid de los Austrias contains some of the most atmospheric parts of the city, a rich array of architectural and artistic treasures – including the lavish Royal Palace – and dozens of great bars and eateries.

LAVAPIÉS AND EMBAJADORES

The areas south of Plaza Mayor were originally tough, working-class districts whose character has changed in recent years as the inhabitants become younger and more cosmopolitan, the districts more fashionable, and the bars and restaurants more enticing.

SOL, SANTA ANA AND HUERTAS

The major attraction for most visitors to this, the bustling heart of Madrid, is its beautiful bars and lively nightlife, though the area is also famed for its historic connections with art and literature.

THE PASEO DEL ARTE

Madrid's three world-class art galleries, the Prado, the Thyssen-Bornemisza and the Centro de Arte Reina Sofía, together form what is known as the Paseo del

▼ The Prado

Arte and offer an unmissable attraction for any visitor.

EL RETIRO

The delightful and popular Retiro park is the perfect place to relax and unwind away from the bustle of the city.

GRAN VÍA

One of Madrid's main thoroughfares and lined with monumental buildings, Gran Vía is also the southern border of Chueca, the focal point of Madrid's gay scene, and bohemian Malasaña, both of which contain an amazing concentration of bars, cafés, restaurants and nightlife.

BARRIO DE SALAMANCA

Exclusive Barrio de Salamanca contains some of Madrid's smartest restaurants and most of the city's designer shops, and is also home of Real Madrid's Santiago Bernabéu stadium.

TOLEDO AND SEGOVIA

Two of Spain's most splendid historic cities are within easy reach of the capital. Immortalized by El Greco, Toledo remains one of the country's most enchanting places, while Segovia is famed for its fabulous architecture, magnificent mountain setting and outstanding Castilian cuisine.

▼ Calle Alcalá and Gran Vía

Ideas

The big six

Madrid's legendary nightlife, multitude of bars and tasty tapas have turned the city into a highly popular weekend-break destination, but as well as eating and drinking, no visit to the Spanish capital would be complete without seeing at least some of the big tourist sights. Three magnificent art galleries, a lavish royal palace, a grandiose central plaza and a colossal football stadium are among the must-see attractions for any visitor.

▲ Centro de Arte Reina Sofía

An impressive home for Spain's collection of contemporary art, including Picasso's powerful and emblematic masterpiece *Guernica*.

P.94 ▶ THE PASEO DEL ARTE

▼ Plaza Mayor

Built when the city became Spain's capital in the sixteenth century and once used as a venue for bullfights and executions, Madrid's main square retains an aura of elegance despite the buskers, crowds and somewhat overpriced cafés.

P.49 ▶ PLAZA MAYOR AND MADRID
DE LOS AUSTRIAS

▶ Museo del Prado

One of the greatest art museums in the world, the Prado contains a fabulous array of work from greats such as El Greco, Titian, Bosch, Rubens, Velázquez and Goya.

P.90 ▶ THE PASEO DEL ARTE

◀ Museo Thyssen-Bornemisza

An outstanding collection assembled by the Thyssen-Bornemisza dynasty that provides an unprecedented excursion through the history of Western art.

P.93 ▶ THE PASEO DEL ARTE

▼ Palacio Real

Marvel at the magnificent, over-the-top decor in this one-time royal residence now used only for ceremonial purposes.

P.60 ▶ THE PALACIO REAL AND ÓPERA

▼ Estadio Santiago Bernabéu

Home to Real Madrid and venue for the 1982 World Cup final, a tour of this awesome stadium is a must for any football fan. Better still, take in a game.

P.122 ▶ SALAMANCA AND THE PASEO DE LA CASTELLANA

Kids' Madrid

Children are doted on throughout Spain and the capital is no exception. Kids are welcome at virtually all cafés and restaurants, though you may have to change your child's bedtime schedule if you want to find somewhere for an evening meal. As for sights, Madrid may lack the child-specific attractions of other European capitals, but there's still plenty to keep youngsters occupied and interested during a short stay, from parks and zoos to cable cars and funfairs.

▲ Museo de Ferrocarril

With its intriguing collection of model railways and impressive array of full-size locomotives, the railway museum will hold the interest of most children and many parents too.

P.74 ▸ THE RASTRO, LAVAPIÉS AND EMBAJADORES

▲ The Teléferico

For a bird's-eye view of the city, take the cable car across the Manzanares river to the middle of the Casa de Campo park.

P.133 ▸ PLAZA DE ESPAÑA AND BEYOND

▼ Madrid's Zoo

Casa de Campo is home to an attractively laid-out zoo whose child-pleasing animal attractions include lions, bears, koalas, sharks and an extensive collection of reptiles.

P.134 ▶ PLAZA DE ESPAÑA AND BEYOND

▲ Parque de Atracciones

Of the many rides at this popular theme park, kids will love the log flume, while teenagers might prefer the white-water rapids ride and the stomach-churning thrills of the Abismo rollercoaster.

P.135 ▶ PLAZA DE ESPAÑA AND BEYOND

▶ The Retiro

The large, city-centre Retiro park has, with its play areas, puppet shows, duck ponds and boating lake, enough to allow kids to burn off some excess energy – and plenty of snack bars to refuel.

P.98 ▶ THE RETIRO AND AROUND

▼ Casa de Campo

Wilder and less accessible than the Retiro, the Casa de Campo, with its boating lake, play areas and popular summer swimming pool, is an ideal place to let off steam.

P.134 ▶ PLAZA DE ESPAÑA AND BEYOND

After dark

Madrid's renowned late-night scene took off with La Movida Madrileña in the late 1970s when the end of the Franco era released a long-suppressed desire to indulge in pure hedonistic enjoyment. Things have mellowed since, but the city still has a dizzying variety of nighttime attractions from chic cocktail spots and cool discobares, to tapas specialists and even a late-night, chocolate-lover's heaven that is a Madrileño institution.

▼ El Chicote

For a relaxing late-night cocktail, follow in the footsteps of celebrities and try the Art Deco *El Chicote*.

P.117 ▶ GRAN VÍA, CHUECA AND MALASAÑA

▼ Chocolatería de San Ginés

The traditional way to end a night on the tiles is to have a *chocolate con churros* (thick hot chocolate with deep-fried hoops of batter) at the city's most famous *chocolatería*.

P.67 ▶ THE PALACIO REAL AND ÓPERA

▲ Santa Ana

Well-established and hugely popular drinking and eating zone around a vibrant plaza. Your only difficulty will be deciding which bar to visit next.

P.78 ▸ SOL, SANTA ANA AND HUERTAS

◀ Drag queens

Drag queens are a feature of many of the leading Madrid nightspots and for a spot of dinner with your divas, the popular *Gula Gula* restaurant is your place.

P.115 ▸ GRAN VÍA, CHUECA AND MALASAÑA

▼ Clubbing

Madrid has a massive range of clubs, from unpretentious discobares to serious cutting-edge dance venues.

P.117 ▸ GRAN VÍA, CHUECA AND MALASAÑA

Green spaces

In complete contrast to its narrow, people-and-traffic-filled streets, Madrid boasts more green spaces than any other European capital. Whether you want a formal English-style garden, a semi-wilderness on the city's doorstep or an indoor rainforest, Madrid provides many welcome escapes from the urban hustle and bustle.

▲ Atocha station tropical garden

Contained in an elegant nineteenth-century station and with a constant mist of water enveloping its tropical plants, this garden provides a surreal backdrop to the more mundane activities of this busy railway terminus.

P.102 ▶ THE RETIRO AND AROUND

▲ Jardines Botánicos

Dating back to the eighteenth century, the botanical gardens form an amazingly tranquil oasis alongside the busy Paseo del Prado.

P.100 ▶ THE RETIRO AND AROUND

▼ Parque del Oeste

Redesigned after being devastated during the Civil War, the Parque del Oeste contains a pretty ornamental stream, assorted statues, a fragrant rose garden and even a genuine Egyptian temple.

P.133 ▸ PLAZA DE ESPAÑA AND BEYOND

▲ Campo del Moro

One of the city's most beautiful parks is also one of its most underused, but this allows you to enjoy even more the shady paths, ornamental pools and magnificent views up to the Palacio Real.

P.62 ▸ THE PALACIO REAL AND ÓPERA

◀ Casa de Campo

Once part of the royal hunting estate, Casa de Campo is the wildest and biggest of the city's parks, featuring mountain-bike trails, a jogging track, tennis courts and a huge lake.

P.134 ▸ PLAZA DE ESPAÑA AND BEYOND

▶ The Retiro

Once privately owned by the royal family, this city-centre park has become Madrileños' favourite play-ground, with a boating lake and a crystal palace hosting regular exhibitions among its attractions.

P.98 ▸ THE RETIRO AND AROUND

18

Shopping

From a ramshackle flea market and eccentric local shops specializing in religious bric-a-brac, to food markets and exclusive designer outlets, Madrid provides something for both casual browsers and dedicated shopaholics alike. For fashion, the smartest addresses are in and around Salamanca, while Chueca and Malasaña are the places to go for street wear and shoes. The area south of Plaza Mayor is full of fascinating traditional establishments and antiques can be picked up in the galleries near the Rastro.

▲ The Rastro

Though better on atmosphere than bargains, it's worth dragging yourself out of bed for the famous Sunday-morning Rastro flea market.

P.70 ▸ THE RASTRO, LAVAPIÉS
AND EMBAJADORES

▲ Calle Postas

For off-beat and eccentric souvenirs, you can't beat the quirky little shops that line the small streets near the Plaza Mayor.

P.50 ▸ PLAZA MAYOR AND
MADRID DE LOS AUSTRIAS

▼ Flamenco Vive

All things flamenco from frilly dresses and castanets, to CDs and guitars. A fascinating place to visit even if you have no intention of buying anything.

P.66 ▸ THE PALACIO REAL AND ÓPERA

▲ Salamanca designer stores

The upmarket Salamanca district is home to some of the city's most exclusive – and expensive – designer outlets.

P.124 ▸ SALAMANCA AND THE PASEO DE LA CASTELLANA

◀ Calle Fuencarral

If the nightlife bug bites and you need the latest fashions to complete your look, Calle Fuencarral is the place to come.

P.113 ▸ GRAN VÍA, CHUECA AND MALASAÑA

▼ Caramelos Paco

Selling every conceivable type of sugary delight, the only problem you'll have in this old-fashioned sweet shop is knowing when to stop.

P.55 ▸ PLAZA MAYOR AND MADRID DE LOS AUSTRIAS

The big three art galleries

With three celebrated art galleries lying within a kilometre of each other in the city centre, Madrid can justifiably claim to be "European capital of art". The Prado is the top attraction with the Thyssen an ideal complement, while the Reina Sofía is the gallery of choice for those who like their art modern. It would be an impossible task to list all of the museums' highlights, but here are six outstanding pieces, worthy of everyone's attention.

▲ Velázquez's Las Meninas

Velázquez's magnum opus has captivated all who have seen it and is rightfully given pride of place in the Prado.

P.90 ▶ THE PASEO DEL ARTE

▼ Holbein's Henry VIII

The fabulous array of art on show at the Thyssen-Bornemisza includes a superlative collection of Renaissance portraits as exemplified by Holbein's renowned depiction of the notorious English monarch.

P.93 ▶ THE PASEO DEL ARTE

▲ Picasso's Guernica

Picasso's masterpiece is the jewel in the crown of the Reina Sofía's stunning collection of contemporary art.

P.94 ▸ THE PASEO DEL ARTE

▶ The Garden of Earthly Delights

The Prado houses the very best of Bosch's macabre and hallucinogenic work.

P.90 ▸ THE PASEO DEL ARTE

▼ Goya's Black Paintings

The haunting series of works painted by the deaf and embittered Goya are one of the highlights of any visit to the Prado.

P.92 ▸ THE PASEO DEL ARTE

Architecture and landmarks

Madrid is home to a hotch-potch of architectural styles reflecting the city's haphazard growth and chequered history. Moorish rule, the arrival of the Habsburgs, the invasion of the French, the Franco dictatorship and the new democratic era have all left their stamp on the capital's architecture. There are also a handful of memorable landmarks dotted around the city centre that are worth searching out.

▲ Plaza de Colón

Cristobal Colón, or Christopher Columbus as he's known to English speakers, is honoured by a monument to him in an eponymous square.

P.119 ▸ SALAMANCA AND THE PASEO DE LA CASTELLANA

▼ Puerta de Europa

The sloping smoked-glass towers known as the Puerta de Europa provide a dramatic flourish towards the end of the Paseo de la Castellana.

P.123 ▸ SALAMANCA AND THE PASEO DE LA CASTELLANA

◀ Terminal 4 at Barajas

The eye-catching Richard Rogers terminal 4 building at Barajas airport is just one of a new generation of buildings, designed by high-profile architects, that now litter the Madrid cityscape.

P.175 ▸ ESSENTIALS

▶ Puerta de Alcalá

The huge monumental gate next to the Retiro once marked the eastern edge of the city, and today it's become one of Madrid's most emblematic landmarks.

P.100 ▸ THE RETIRO AND AROUND

▼ Edificio Metrópolis

The French-designed building at the junction of Gran Vía and Calle Alcalá is one of the city's most stylish constructions.

P.107 ▸ GRAN VÍA, CHUECA AND MALASAÑA

▲ Palacio de Comunicaciones

For sheer architectural extravagance, it's hard to beat the former central post office and future home to the local council, the aptly named Palace of Communications.

P.82 ▸ SOL, SANTA ANA AND HUERTAS

Madrid people

Largely a city of immigrants it's difficult to find a person whose real roots are in Madrid, but its status as capital has meant that a string of personalities have made it their home and left their mark on its history, from kings who transformed it into the headquarters of a global empire to movie directors who helped put Madrid on the international map by committing the city's idiosyncrasies to film.

▼ Miguel Cervantes

Playwright, soldier and author of *Don Quixote*, Cervantes lived in the Huertas area and was buried in the convent of Las Trinitarias Descalzas. He is now commemorated by an imposing monument in Plaza de España.

P.129 ▶ THE PLAZA DE ESPAÑA AND BEYOND

▼ Goya

The precursor of modern painting, Francisco de Goya lived and worked in Madrid from the late eighteenth until the early nineteenth century, documenting the often tumultuous events played out during his lifetime.

P.92 ▶ THE PASEO DEL ARTE

▲ San Isidro

A humble agricultural labourer renowned for his pious devotion and generosity, Madrid's patron saint, San Isidro, is remembered in an annual series of fiestas.

P.54 ▸ PLAZA MAYOR AND
MADRID DE LOS AUSTRIAS

▲ Pedro Almodóvar

The enfant terrible of Spanish cinema made his name during the *Movida Madrileña* in the late 1970s and early 1980s before going on to Oscar-winning success with *Hable con ella* (*Talk to her*) and *Todo sobre mi madre* (*All about my mother*).

P.180 ▸ ESSENTIALS

▼ Felipe II

It was Felipe II, Spain's most famous and powerful king, who decided to base the formerly itinerant court in Madrid in 1561, making it the nerve centre of his imperial rule.

P.138 ▸ EL ESCORIAL AND VALLE
DE LOS CAÍDOS

▼ Franco

After his victory in the 1936–39 Civil War, General Franco dominated Spanish life for forty years, running his dictatorship from his El Pardo residence on the outskirts of the capital.

P.135 ▸ PLAZA DE ESPAÑA AND
BEYOND

Castizo Madrid

Castizo refers to anything that is viewed as authentically Madrileño, whether it be the people, the food or the fiestas. Akin to London's cockneys, castizos are the straight-talking, no-nonsense locals who hail from barrios like Lavapiés. During the summer fiestas the men can be seen dressed up in dogtooth waistcoats, neckerchiefs and flat caps, the women In long, tight-fitting frilly dresses.

▲ La Corrala

La Corrala is one of the few surviving traditional tenement blocks that used to litter the poorer barrios of the city. This one has been preserved and acts as a backdrop to the summer *zarzuelas* in Lavapiés.

P.71 ▸ THE RASTRO, LAVAPIÉS AND EMBAJADORES

▲ Taberna Angel Sierra

One of the city's great watering holes with a beautiful tiled frontage looking out on to Plaza Chueca. This is the place to come for an *apertivo* of *vermút* or beer before Sunday lunch.

P.117 ▸ GRAN VÍA, CHUECA AND MALASAÑA

▲ Botín

Claiming to be the oldest restaurant in the world, *Botín* was one of Hemingway's hangouts, while Goya was allegedly employed as a dishwasher at one time. Specializes in Castilian roasts.

P.56 ▸ PLAZA MAYOR AND MADRID DE LOS AUSTRIAS

▼ La Bola

Established in the late nineteenth century, *La Bola* specializes in the traditional Madrileño speciality *cocido*, a warming and extremely filling meat and chickpea stew.

P.67 ▸ PALACIO REAL AND ÓPERA

▲ Castizo shops

There are a host of traditional shops selling everything from flamenco guitars to haberdashery clustered around Sol and Santa Ana. Seseña has been around since the start of the last century and specializes in traditional Madrileño capes.

P.83 ▸ SOL, SANTA ANA AND HUERTAS

◀ Summer Verbenas

When the Madrid heat is at its peak, the locals, many in traditional costume, part on the streets of La Latina and Lavapié celebrate the festivals of San Cayetar Lorenzo and La Virgen de la Paloma

P.179 ▸ ESSENTIALS

Eating

Eating out in Madrid is one of the highlights of a visit to the city and there's something to suit every pocket and taste. From back-street bars to high-class designer restaurants and with a bewildering array of cuisines encompassing tapas, traditional Madrileño, Spanish regional and international dishes, there is no excuse to go home disappointed. In a city that has often been an intimidating destination for vegetarians, there is now a growing number of restaurants offering attractive alternatives to meat.

▲ New wave restaurants

Mezklum is just one of a new generation of design-conscious restaurants that have sprung up all over the city. Fusion-style food, minimalist decor and a young clientele are the trademarks of most of these eateries.

P.85 ▶ SOL, SANTA ANA AND HUERTAS

▲ Casa Mingo

Cheap, cheerful and very tasty. Try the spit-roast chicken and Asturian cider at this classic restaurant down by the Manzanares.

P.136 ▶ PLAZA DE ESPAÑA AND BEYOND

▲ Tapas

For an authentic night out eating tapas, forget staying in one place and instead copy the locals and sample the house speciality as you hop from bar to bar.

P.86 ▸ SOL, SANTA ANA AND HUERTAS

▼ The Museo de Jamón

Packed to the rafters with cured hams, this is an ideal place to sample one of Spain's great delicacies.

P.87 ▸ SOL, SANTA ANA AND HUERTAS

▲ Casa del Abuelo

A fabulous little bar serving up a constant supply of fried prawns accompanied by sweet red wine or a cool beer.

P.86 ▸ SOL, SANTA ANA AND HUERTAS

▼ Posada de la Villa

One of several old coaching inns that line Cava Baja, serving up excellent Castilian roasts in a traditional atmosphere.

P.57 ▸ PLAZA MAYOR AND MADRID DE LOS AUSTRIAS

Drinking

Bars and cafés are a central feature of Madrileño life and there's an incredible variety to choose from, including cervecerías (beer specialists), coctelerías (cocktail bars), champagnerías (champagne bars), tabernas (old-style taverns), bares de copas (bars mainly serving spirits), and, inevitably, a host of Irish pubs. As for coffee, steer clear of the franchised chains and head for a traditional café for a much tastier brew.

▼ Viva Madrid

A classic on the Madrileño nightlife circuit – arrive early to admire the beautiful tiles and vaulted roof before the crowds pour in.

P.88 ▶ SOL, SANTA ANA AND HUERTAS

▼ Drinking granizado or horchata in the Retiro

Granizado (crushed ice with lemon, orange or coffee) and *horchata* (a milky drink made from tiger nuts) are two favourite summer refreshments.

P.98 ▶ THE RETIRO AND AROUND

▲ Cocktails at Del Diego

Sample some of the best cocktails in town at this cool and stylish bar just behind Gran Vía.

P.117 ▸ GRAN VÍA, CHUECA AND MALASAÑA

◀ La Venencia

A rather dingy-looking bar from the outside, but inside you'll find a wonderful range of Spanish sherries, one of the country's traditional aperitifs.

P.88 ▸ SOL, SANTA ANA AND HUERTAS

▼ Coffee culture

There's no better way to kick-start the day than a cup of coffee – or two – at one of the city's traditional cafés.

P.113 ▸ GRAN VÍA, CHUECA AND MALASAÑA

Sport and culture

Although Madrileños certainly know how to let their hair down, they also have an insatiable appetite for culture and sport. Cinema, *zarzuela* (light opera), classical concerts and flamenco are all firmly established in the capital, while for sports fans two of the country's biggest football clubs have their homes here. For many Spaniards bullfighting is the ultimate spectacle and for those with a genuine interest, Madrid hosts one of the most prestigious taurine festivals every May.

▲ Atlético Madrid

More down-to-earth than neighbours Real, Atlético are still one of the country's biggest clubs.

P.71 ▸ THE RASTRO, LAVAPIÉS AND EMBAJADORES

▼ Real Madrid

David Beckham and the "galacticos" may have gone, but catching a game at Real Madrid's splendid Bernabéu stadium is still a must for any sports fan. If you can't get to a game, the stadium tour is the next best thing.

P.122 ▸ SALAMANCA AND THE PASEO DE LA CASTELLANA

▼ Bullfighting

For a few weeks in the year during the prestigious San Isidro festival in May, Las Ventas ring in Madrid becomes the bullfighting capital of the world.

P.124 ▶ SALAMANCA AND THE PASEO DE LA CASTELLANA

▲ Teatro Real

The lavish refurbishment of the nineteenth-century Teatro Real has left the city with a magnificent venue for operas, ballets and classical concerts.

P.64 ▶ THE PALACIO REAL AND ÓPERA

▼ Flamenco

Andalucía may be the home of flamenco, but some of the best acts can be appreciated on the Madrid scene.

P.76 ▶ THE RASTRO, LAVAPIÉS AND EMBAJADORES

Specialist museums

Although the big three art galleries dominate the tourist agenda, Madrid is also home to a host of less famous, smaller-scale museums. From fascinating displays on the life of a specific artist or writer to national collections with unique exhibits, these specialist spaces can be just as rewarding as their big-name counterparts.

▲ Real Academia de Bellas Artes

It may not be able to boast the heavyweight attractions of the big three art galleries, but the Royal Academy of Fine Art contains some captivating work by Goya, El Greco, José de Ribera and Zurbarán.

P.81 ▶ SOL, SANTA ANA AND HUERTAS

▼ Museo Sorolla

This atmospheric tribute to the life and work of the artist Sorolla – often called the "Spanish Impressionist" – is housed in his beautifully preserved former residence just off the Castellana.

P.121 ▶ SALAMANCA AND THE PASEO DE LA CASTELLANA

▶ Real Fábrica de Tapices

The Royal Tapestry Factory is both a fascinating museum and a thriving workshop, allowing visitors the chance to view works in progress and see some of the *fábrica*'s historic finished pieces.

P.103 ▶ THE RETIRO AND
AROUND

35

◀ Museo Arqueológico Nacional

The Celto-Iberian bust known as the *Dama de Elche* is probably the museum's most famous artefact, but it also contains some highly impressive Visigothic, Roman, Greek and Egyptian finds.

P.121 ▶ SALAMANCA AND
THE PASEO DE LA
CASTELLANA

▶ Museo Lázaro Galdiano

A treasure-trove of paintings, furniture and objets d'art in this outstanding personal collection assembled by publisher and businessman José Lázaro Galdiano.

P.122 ▶ SALAMANCA AND THE
PASEO DE LA CASTELLANA

▼ Casa de Lope de Vega

A delightful little museum set in the reconstructed home and garden of the prolific, seventeenth-century Spanish writer.

P.79 ▶ SOL, SANTA ANA AND
HUERTAS

Out of the city

Madrid has enough attractions to keep you busy for days, but within easy reach of the capital are several alluring sights should you need a break from the big city. Toledo and Segovia, two of Spain's most captivating historic cities, are top day-trip choices, or there's Felipe II's stunning mountain-side palace-mausoleum complex of El Escorial, the riverside oasis of Aranjuez with its lavish Baroque palace, and Franco's former residence at El Pardo to choose from.

▲ Segovia

Segovia is brimming with outstanding architectural monuments including a sumptuous cathedral and remarkable Roman aqueduct.

P.155 ▶ SEGOVIA

◀ El Escorial

Part monastery, part mausoleum and part palace, Felipe II's mammoth construction is the awesome architectural legacy of Spain's most powerful monarch.

P.138 ▸ EL ESCORIAL AND VALLE DE LOS CAÍDOS

◀ El Pardo

The royal hunting lodge where Franco had his headquarters contains the Caudillo's old cabinet rooms, the theatre where he used to censor films and the chapel where he prayed.

P.135 ▸ PLAZA DE ESPAÑA AND BEYOND

▲ Aranjuez

Visit the palace, stroll around the gardens and enjoy the delicious local strawberries at this verdant riverside escape, once a spring-time residence of the Spanish royal family.

P.142 ▸ ARANJUEZ AND CHINCHÓN

▶ Toledo

With its hill-top location, imposing cathedral and beautiful historical core, Toledo is one of the most dramatic Spanish cities. Try to avoid the summer heat and the weekend crowds though.

P.147 ▸ TOLEDO

Madrid calendar

Madrid has a calendar of celebrations to rival many other Spanish cities. Most events have a religious origin and celebrate some local saint or other, but Madrileños know how to party, and food and drink play an integral part in all festivities. Another bonus is that events are always open to visitors and provide a great way of getting a real understanding of what makes the city tick.

▲ Carnaval

The pre-Lent blow-out of *Carnaval* is celebrated with special enthusiasm in Chueca, but there are costume parades all over the city, finishing off with the peculiar Burial of the Sardine in the Paseo de la Florida.

P.179 ▸ ESSENTIALS

▼ San Isidro

The week-long festivals to celebrate the city's patron saint see music, dance and festivities across Madrid.

P.179 ▸ ESSENTIALS

▲ Christmas

Christmas is a full two-week affair in Spain, ending with a huge procession of the Three Kings in the city centre on the evening of January 5.

`P.179` ▸ ESSENTIALS

▼ Dos de Mayo

Centred in and around the Malasaña plaza of the same name, these fiestas commemorate the popular rebellion against French occupation in 1808.

`P.179` ▸ ESSENTIALS

◄ Semana Santa

Though not as dramatic as in Andalucía, Madrid's and Toledo's Easter week processions are still an impressive and moving sight.

`P.179` ▸ ESSENTIALS

Gay and lesbian Madrid

Recent years have witnessed an explosion in the gay and lesbian scene in Madrid. The area around Plaza Chueca remains at the heart of the action, but clubs have sprung up in other areas too, and there are plenty of shops, cafés, bars and events catering for the city's gay inhabitants. Once highly conservative, Spanish society now takes a generally liberal attitude towards gay rights and issues.

▲ Café Acuarela

Baroque decor, highly drinkable cocktails and a cosy atmosphere make this one of Chueca's most popular cafés.

P.113 ▸ GRAN VÍA, CHUECA AND MALASAÑA

▲ Liquid

Stylish bar favoured by an ultra-cool gay crowd.

P.117 ▸ GRAN VÍA, CHUECA AND MALASAÑA

▲ Berkana bookshop

One of the best sources of information for all that's happening on the Madrid gay scene.

P.181 ▸ ESSENTIALS

▶ Plaza Chueca

Centre of the Chueca gay scene, this plaza is always packed with people spilling out from the surrounding bars, restaurants and clubs.

P.109 ▸ GRAN VÍA, CHUECA AND MALASAÑA

▼ Gay Pride March

Gay Pride Day at the end of June triggers a week of partying, processions and celebrations all around Chueca.

P.179 ▸ ESSENTIALS

Religious buildings

In a country with such a strong religious tradition it's hardly surprising that the Catholic Church has left its mark on the Spanish capital. Churches, chapels, monasteries and convents pepper the city and, behind often rather modest facades, many conceal remarkable artistic treasures and religious relics. Most places are either free to enter or make a modest charge, but appropriate dress and behaviour are expected.

▲ Almudena Cathedral

Taking over a century to complete, the city's cathedral is imposing rather than beautiful. Inaugurated by Pope John Paul II in 1993, it was the venue of the recent wedding of heir to the throne Prince Felipe.

P.61 ▸ THE PALACIO REAL AND
ÓPERA

▲ La Ermita de San Antonio

The stunning Goya frescoes that decorate this tiny Greek-cross church provide an appropriate tribute to the artist whose remains are housed within.

P.134 ▸ PLAZA DE ESPAÑA AND
BEYOND

▼ Monasterio de las Descalzas Reales

An array of exquisite artworks lies within this former medieval palace that remains a working convent to this day.

P.65 ▶ THE PALACIO REAL AND ÓPERA

▼ San Pedro el Viejo

One of the oldest churches in the city, San Pedro features a fourteenth-century Mudéjar tower.

P.53 ▶ PLAZA MAYOR AND MADRID DE LOS AUSTRIAS

▲ San Francisco el Grande

After a lengthy renovation, the magnificent chapels and frescoed cupola of this enormous church can be seen in something close to their original glory.

P.55 ▶ PLAZA MAYOR AND MADRID DE LOS AUSTRIAS

▲ Iglesia de San Andrés

Badly damaged in the Civil War, much of this church has been restored in recent years, including the fine brick cupola and the richly decorated interior.

P.54 ▶ PLAZA MAYOR AND MADRID DE LOS AUSTRIAS

Plazas

Madrid has a range of plazas large and small, ranging from the refined elegance of the Plaza Mayor to the down-to-earth cosmopolitanism of Lavapiés. Ideal for a well-earned rest and some Madrileño people-watching, many are also home to excellent bars, terrazas and restaurants.

▲ Plaza de Oriente

An aristocratic, tree-lined space, bordered on one side by the Royal Palace and on the other by the Teatro Real and the stylish *Café Oriente*.

P.63 ▸ THE PALACIO REAL AND ÓPERA

▼ Plaza de Lavapiés

Lavapiés is an animated multicultural barrio with a host of popular bars and cafés.

P.72 ▸ THE RASTRO, LAVAPIÉS AND EMBAJADORES

▶ Plaza Santa Ana

Bar-laden square that's the focal point of the Huertas nightlife scene.

P.78 ▸ SOL, SANTA ANA AND HUERTAS

◀ Plaza Mayor

Brainchild of Felipe II, Madrid's main square has had an eventful, sometimes bloodthirsty history, but today offers an atmospheric backdrop for a relaxing drink.

P.49 ▸ PLAZA MAYOR AND MADRID DE LOS AUSTRIAS

▼ Plaza de España

Big, brash and busy, Plaza de España was part of Franco's attempt to prove that Spain was a modern, go-ahead country by the 1950s.

P.129 ▸ PLAZA DE ESPAÑA AND BEYOND

▼ Plaza de la Villa

Madrid's oldest square was once the focus of the medieval city and still houses several local government offices.

P.52 ▸ PLAZA MAYOR AND MADRID DE LOS AUSTRIAS

Places

Plaza Mayor and Madrid de los Austrias

Named after the royal family and their original homeland, the district known as Madrid de los Austrias, or Habsburg Madrid, contains some of the oldest and most atmospheric parts of the city. Centred around the suitably grandiose Plaza Mayor, the area is made up of a twisting grid of streets, filled with Flemish-inspired architecture of red brick and grey stone. Most visitors only make it to the Plaza Mayor and its over-priced cafés and restaurants, but there are appealing sights scattered throughout the area, especially in the characterful barrio (district) of La Latina, which stretches south of the square. This region is also home to some of the city's best restaurants, tapas bars and flamenco tablaos, especially around calles Almendro, Cava Baja and Cava Alta.

Plaza Mayor

The splendidly theatrical Plaza Mayor was originally the brainchild of Felipe II who, in the late sixteenth century, wanted to construct a more prestigious focus for his new capital. The **Casa de la Panadería** on the north side of the square is the oldest building, dating from 1590, but, like much of the plaza, it was rebuilt after fires in the **seventeenth** and eighteenth centuries. The delightful frescoes that adorn the facade were only added in 1992. Today it houses the municipal tourist office (daily 9.30am–8.30pm).

Capable of holding up to fifty thousand people, the square was used for state occasions, autos-de-fé (public trials of heretics followed, more often than not, by burning of the victims) and executions, jousts, plays and bullfights. The large bronze equestrian statue in the middle is of Felipe III and dates from 1616.

Today, Plaza Mayor is primarily a tourist haunt, full of expensive outdoor cafés and restaurants that advertise themselves as "typical Spanish" – best to stick to a drink here. However, an air of grandeur clings to the place, and the plaza still hosts a range of public functions from outdoor theatre and music, to Christmas

▼ PLAZA MAYOR

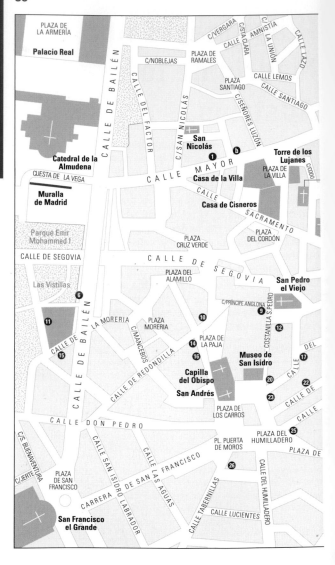

fairs and a Sunday stamp and coin market.

South of the plaza, the narrow streets hold some of the city's oldest *mesones* (taverns), where an early evening drink allows you to soak up the atmosphere.

Leading off the northeastern corner of the square, Calle Postas is known for its shops selling all manner of religious articles, from dog collars and habits to rosary beads and plastic models of the baby Jesus.

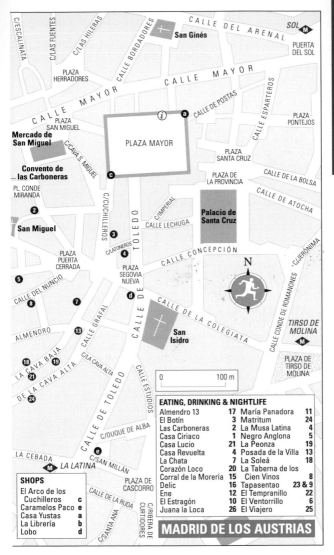

EATING, DRINKING & NIGHTLIFE

Almendro 13	17	María Panadora	11
El Botín	3	Matritum	24
Las Carboneras	2	La Musa Latina	4
Casa Ciriaco	1	Negro Anglona	5
Casa Lucio	21	La Peonza	19
Casa Revuelta	4	Posada de la Villa	13
La Chata	7	La Soleá	18
Corazón Loco	20	La Taberna de los	
Corral de la Morería	15	Cien Vinos	8
Delic	16	Tapasentao	23 & 9
Ene	12	El Tempranillo	22
El Estragón	10	El Ventorrillo	6
Juana la Loca	26	El Viajero	25

SHOPS

El Arco de los Cuchilleros	c
Caramelos Paco	e
Casa Yustas	a
La Librería	b
Lobo	d

MADRID DE LOS AUSTRIAS

Calle Mayor

One of the most ancient thoroughfares in the city, Calle Mayor was for centuries the route for religious processions from the Palacio Real to the Monastery of Los Jerónimos.

The street is home to a variety of little shops and bars and is flanked by the facades of some of the most evocative buildings in the city. Set back from the road, near the entrance to the Plaza Mayor, is the splendid decorative ironwork of the **Mercado de San Miguel**, built in 1916 and until recently a thriving market although it is now closed for renovation.

Of Calle Mayor's magnificent early twentieth-century apartment blocks, it's worth stopping off at no. 84, the **Casa Ciriaco** (see p.56), for a wine or a coffee. This traditional *taberna* is full of memorabilia detailing the colourful history of the building, in particular the notorious attack on the royal wedding procession of Alfonso XIII and his English bride, Victoria Eugenie, in 1906. A bomb, secreted in a bunch of flowers, was thrown from one of the second-floor balconies, killing 23 onlookers but leaving the royal couple unscathed.

San Nicolás de los Servitas

Plaza de San Nicolás 1. Mon 8.30am–1.30pm & 5.30–9pm, Tues–Sat 8.30–9.30am & 6.30–9pm, Sun 9.30am–2pm & 6.30–9pm. Largely

▼ PLAZA DE LA VILLA

rebuilt between the fifteenth and seventeenth centuries, this, Madrid's oldest church, still includes a twelfth-century Mudéjar tower featuring traditional Arabic horseshoe arches. Inside is a very small but interesting display on the history of Muslim Madrid. Juan de Herrera, architect of El Escorial (see p.138), is buried in the crypt.

Plaza de la Villa

This charming plaza, just off Calle Mayor, provides a showcase for three centuries of Spanish architectural development. The oldest buildings are the simple but eye-catching fifteenth-century **Torre y Casa de Los Lujanes** where Francis I of France is said to have been imprisoned in 1525 after his capture at the Battle of Pavia. On the south side of the square is the **Casa de Cisneros**, constructed for the nephew of Cardinal Cisneros (early sixteenth-century Inquisitor-General and Regent of Spain) in the Plateresque style, incorporating the intricate techniques of silversmiths or *plateros* (hence Plateresque). It now houses the Mayor of Madrid's offices.

The remaining side of the square is taken up by the **Casa de la Villa**, one of the most important and emblematic buildings of Habsburg Madrid. It was constructed in stages during the seventeenth century to house the offices and records of the council. The initial design by Juan Gómez de Mora wasn't completed until 1693, 45 years after his death, and was mellowed by the addition of Baroque details in the eighteenth century. The weekly tour (5pm every Mon;

free) is normally only in Spanish but is still well worth it to get a peek inside. The Patio de Los Cristales contains a stunning stained-glass roof depicting some of the city's most celebrated sights, but the highlight of the tour is the Salón de Plenos or Assembly Room, where meetings of the council still take place. The chamber drips with gold leaf and is lavishly decorated with burgundy velvet curtains, red leather benches and frescoes by Antonio Palomino.

▲ SWEETS FROM LAS CARBONERAS CONVENT

Convento de las Carboneras

Plaza Conde de Miranda 3. Founded in the early seventeenth century, this convent belongs to the closed Hieronymite Order. It's famous for the biscuits and cakes it makes and sells – a tradition in Spanish convents since the time of St Teresa of Ávila, who gave out sweetened egg yolks to the poor – that can be purchased every day 9.30am–1pm and 4–6.30pm. Ring the bell above the sign reading *venta de dulces* to be let in, then follow the signs to the *torno*; the business takes place by means of a revolving drum to preserve the closed nature of the order.

Basílica de San Miguel

C/San Justo 4. July–Sept 14 Mon–Sat 9.45am–1pm & 6–9pm, Sun 9.40am–1.40pm & 6.30–9pm; Sept 15–June 30 Mon–Sat 9.45am–2pm & 5.30–9pm, Sun 9.40am–2.40pm & 6–9pm. Standing amongst a host of other graceful buildings – most of which house local government offices – San Miguel stands out as one of the few examples of a full-blown Baroque church in Madrid. Designed at the end of the seventeenth century for Don Luis, the precocious 5-year-old Archbishop of Toledo and youngest son of Felipe V, its features include an unconventional convex facade with four recesses, each containing a statue, variously representing Charity, Strength, Faith and Hope.

San Pedro el Viejo

Costanilla de San Pedro. Mon–Sat 9am–noon & 6–8pm, Sun 9am–1pm. Free. At the heart of busy La Latina is the Mudéjar tower of San Pedro El Viejo. The second-oldest church in Madrid, it's said to have been founded in the fourteenth century by Alfonso XI, and stands on the site of an old mosque, though most of the church was rebuilt in the seventeenth century.

Plaza de la Paja

One of the real gems of old Madrid, this ancient sloping plaza was the commercial and civic hub of the city before the construction of the Plaza Mayor, and was once surrounded by a series of mansions owned by local dignitaries. With the restored houses beaming down on the former market square, this is one of the few areas in the city where you can get a break from the interminable Madrid traffic while having a drink at one of several bars. At the bottom is the small Jardin del Príncipe de Anglona (daily: winter 10am–6.30pm; summer 10am–10pm), a survivor of the gardens that used to be attached to the nearby mansions.

Iglesia de San Andrés, Capilla del Obispo and Capilla de San Isidro

Plaza de San Andrés. Mon–Thurs & Sat 8am–1pm & 6–8pm, Fri closed 11.30am–1.30pm, Sun 9am–2pm.

The Iglesia de San Andrés was badly damaged by an anarchist attack in 1936, and the adjoining Capilla del Obispo is still undergoing a long-running renovation programme. However, the main church, whose brick cupola has been restored to its former glory, and the Baroque Capilla de San Isidro are open to visitors. The chapel was built in the mid-seventeenth century to hold the remains of Madrid's patron saint, San Isidro (since moved

▲ IGLESIA DE SAN ANDRÉS

to the Catedral de San Isidro), and the interior is decorated with a beautifully sculpted dome, depicting angels laden with fruit. The lower level – inspired by the pantheon in El Escorial, see p.138 – features a red-marble backdrop, fronted by black columns with gold leaf and sculptures of saints.

Museo de San Isidro

Plaza de San Andrés 2 ⓦwww .munimadrid.es/museosanisidro. Sept–July Tues–Fri 9.30am–8pm, Sat & Sun 10am–2pm; Aug Tues–Sat 9.30am–2.30pm, Sat & Sun 10am–2pm. Free.

Housed in a reconstructed sixteenth-century mansion – supposedly home to San Isidro – this museum includes an informative exhibition on the history of Madrid from prehistoric times up until 1561 (when Felipe II moved the court here on a permanent basis). The archeological collection is in the basement, while the rest of the building is given over to the saint himself, with displays relating to his life and miraculous activities. It also contains a well that was the site of one of his most famous exploits when he rescued his young son, who had plunged headlong into the murky depths, by praying until the waters rose and brought him to the surface again.

The seventeenth-century chapel contained within the museum is built on the spot where the saint was said to have died in 1172.

Parque Emir Mohammed I

Though little more than a scrap of parched land, Parque Emir Mohammed I is notable for its fragments of the city walls that date back to the ninth and twelfth centuries. The park stands next to the Cuesta de la Vega, former site of one of the main entrances to Muslim Madrid, while nearby, the narrow, labyrinthine streets of the former Moorish quarter, La Morería, are still clearly laid out on medieval lines.

San Francisco el Grande

Plaza de San Francisco 11. Tues–Fri 11am–1pm & 4–7pm, Sat 11am–1.30pm; Aug Tues–Sun 11am–12.30pm & 5–7.30pm. €3 with guided tour.

The huge domed church of San Francisco El Grande has had a varied history. The building was completed in 1784, became a national mausoleum in 1837 and reverted to the control of the Franciscan friars in 1926. Now, after a twenty-year restoration programme, it's possible to appreciate this magnificent church in something close to its original glory.

Inside, each of the six chapels is designed in a distinct style ranging from Mozarab and Renaissance to Baroque and Neoclassical. Look out for the early Goya, *The Sermon of San Bernadino of Siena*, in the chapel on your immediate left as you enter, which contains a self-portrait of the 36-year-old artist (in the yellow suit on the right).

Even if your Spanish is not that good, follow the guided tour to get a glimpse of the ante-sacristy with its seventeenth-century Plateresque benches carved from Spanish walnut, and the church's art treasures, including paintings by José de Ribera and Zurbarán.

Shops

El Arco de los Cuchilleros

Plaza Mayor 9. Mon–Sat 11am–8pm, Sun 11am–2.30pm. Though at the heart of tourist Madrid, the goods for sale here are a far cry from the swords, lace and castanets that fill most shops in the area. Crafts include ceramics, leather, wood, jewellery and textiles, and there's a gallery space for exhibitions too. Prices are reasonable and staff helpful.

Caramelos Paco

C/Toledo 55 ⓦ www.caramelospaco .com. Mon–Sat 9.30am–2pm & 5–8pm, Sun 11am–3pm. A child's dream – and a dentist's nightmare – with a window full of every imaginable sugary confection. Giant lollipops, sugar-coated figures and almond-flavoured sticks of rock are among the delights at this old-fashioned sweet shop.

Casa Yustas

Plaza Mayor 30. Mon–Sat 9.30am–9.30pm, Sun 11am–9.30pm. Established in 1894, Madrid's oldest hat shop sells every

▼ CASA YUSTAS

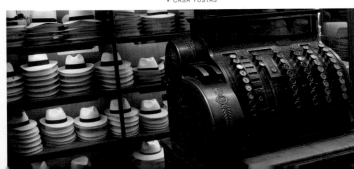

conceivable model from pith helmets and commando berets to panamas and bowlers. There's also a large range of souvenir-style goods, including Lladró porcelain figurines.

La Librería

C/Mayor 80 ⓦ www.edicioneslalibreria .com. Mon–Fri 10am–2pm & 4.30– 7.30pm, Sat 11am–2pm. Tiny place full of books just about Madrid. Most are in Spanish, but many would serve as coffee-table souvenirs. Also a good place to pick up old postcards, historic maps and photos of the city.

Lobo

C/Toledo 30. Mon–Fri 9.45am–1.45pm & 4.30–8pm, Sat 9.45am–1.45pm. Great little old-fashioned shoe shop, selling anything from espadrilles to Menorcan sandals (€24) in every conceivable colour. Particularly good for kids' shoes.

Restaurants

El Botín

C/Cuchilleros 17 ☎913 664 217 ⓦwww.botin.es. Daily 1–4pm & 8pm–midnight. Established in 1725, the highly atmospheric *El Botín* is cited in the *Guinness Book of Records* as Europe's oldest restaurant. Favoured by Hemingway among others, it's inevitably a tourist haunt, but not such a bad one. Highlights are the Castilian roasts – especially *cochinillo* (suckling pig) and *cordero lechal* (lamb). Good house wine too. The autumn and winter only *menú del día* is €35, but you could eat for less.

Casa Ciriaco

C/Mayor 84 ☎915 480 620. Daily except Wed 1–4pm & 8.30–midnight. Closed Aug. Attractive, old-style *taberna*, famous for its traditional Castilian dishes. The *menú* is €20, main dishes a bit less. You can also sample some of the excellent wine in the front bar.

Casa Lucio

C/Cava Baja 35 ☎913 653 252, ⓦwww .casalucio.es. Mon–Fri & Sun 1–4pm & 9pm–midnight, Sat 9pm–midnight. Closed Aug. Madrileños come here for classic Castilian dishes such as

▼ EL BOTÍN

cocido (meaty stew), *callos* (tripe) and roasts, cooked to perfection. Booking is essential and count on around €45 a head.

Ene

C/Nuncio 19 ☎913 662 591, ⓦwww.enerestaurante.com. Mon–Wed 11am–11.30pm, Thurs open till 2am, Fri & Sat till 3am, Sun till midnight. Fashionable bar/ restaurant just below Plaza de la Paja serving a sophisticated, fusion-style €11 *menú del día* and a great €20 brunch at weekends. Cocktails and disc jockeys Thurs–Sun.

El Estragón

Plaza de La Paja 10 ☎913 658 982. Daily 1.30–4pm & 8pm–midnight. With a fine setting on this ancient plaza, this vegetarian restaurant serves the kind of hearty food that non-veggies also enjoy. It does a varied *menú del día* for €10 (dinner *menú* €19), while eating à la carte is a little more expensive. Save space for the desserts.

La Musa Latina

C/Costinilla San Andrés ⓦwww .lamusalatina.com. Mon–Thurs 9am– midnight, Fri 9am–2am, Sat 1pm–2am, Sun 1pm–midnight. Another style-conscious restaurant on the La Latina scene. *La Musa* serves a great value €10 *menú del día*, and a small selection of modern tapas. It has a cool brick-walled bar downstairs with DJ sessions in the evenings.

Negro Anglona

C/Segovia 13 ☎913 663 753, ⓦwww .negroanglona.com. Tues–Thurs & Sun 9pm–1am, Fri & Sat till 2am. All-black decor in this refurbished trendy pasta and pizza joint, situated in the cellars of an old palace. A handy late-night option but service can be slow

at weekends. Expect to pay around €30 a head.

Posada de la Villa

C/Cava Baja 9 ☎913 661 860, ⓦwww.posadadelavilla.com. Mon–Sat 1–4pm & 8pm–midnight, Sun 1–4pm. Closed Aug. The most attractive restaurant in La Latina, spread over three floors of a seventeenth-century coaching inn. Cooking is typically madrileño, including superb roast lamb and a top-notch *cocido*. Reckon on €45 per person for a splurge.

Tapas bars

Almendro 13

C/Almendro 13. Mon–Fri 1–4pm & 7.30pm–midnight, Sat, Sun & hols 1–5pm & 8pm–midnight. Fashionable wood-panelled bar that serves great *fino* sherry from chilled black bottles. Help yourself to the glasses from the racks on the wall and tuck into original tapas of *huevos rotos* (fried eggs on a bed of crisps) and *roscas rellenas* (rings of bread stuffed with various meats).

Casa Revuelta

C/Latoneras 3. Tues–Sat 1–4pm & 8pm–midnight, Sun 1–4pm. A timeless, down-to-earth little bar located in an alleyway just south of Plaza Mayor. It serves an unbeatable tapa of *bacalao frito* (battered cod).

La Chata

C/Cava Baja 24. Daily 2–4.30pm & 8.30pm–12.30am. Closed Tues & Wed lunch time & Sun eve. One of the city's most traditional and popular tiled tapas bars, with hams hanging from the ceiling and taurine and football memorabilia on the walls. Serves a good selection of dishes, including *cebolla rellena* and *pimientos del piquillo rellenos* (stuffed onions and peppers).

Corazón Loco

C/Almendro 22. Noon–1am; Mon & Tues opens at 8pm. The front bar of this popular La Latina watering hole is invariably packed, but there is a quieter, and cosier brick-lined dining area at the back which serves a good range of tapas. Two different set lunches available Tues–Fri for €9 and €12.

Juana la Loca

C/Plaza Puerta de Moros 4. Noon–4.30pm & 8pm–1am. Closed Mon, Sun pm & Aug. Trendy Basque bar serving inventive tapas – *solomillo de avestruz* (ostrich steak) is one of the most popular choices – and very tasty, but fairly pricey, canapés.

Matritum

C/Cava Alta 17. Mon–Fri 8.30pm–midnight, Sat & Sun 1–4.30pm & 8.30pm–midnight. Delicious designer-style tapas, from fig salad with mozarella, anchovies and mint oil to prawn toast with saffron and blackberry sauce. There's an extensive collection of carefully selected wines too.

La Peonza

C/Cava Baja 19. Tues–Sun noon–4pm & 8pm–1am. Friendly bar serving a range of traditional dishes with an imaginative touch including scallops stuffed with crab meat, *gambas al ajillo* (garlic prawns) and a wide range of canapés.

La Taberna de los Cien Vinos

C/Nuncio 16. Tues–Sat 1–3.45pm & 8–11.45pm, Sun 1–3.45pm. A vast array of Spanish wines (every month they sell a different selection) plus plenty of tapas to choose from, including excellent leek pie, smoked salmon and roast beef. Not suitable for the indecisive.

Tapasentao

C/Almendro 27. Tues 8pm–midnight, Wed, Thurs & Fri 1–4.30pm & 8pm–midnight, Sat & Sun 1pm–2am, Sun 1pm–midnight. Closed second half Aug. Fill in a card ticking your choices from the imaginatively presented, very tasty and reasonably priced dishes. Recommended are the excellent asparagus in avocado sauce, *chorizo* with wafer-thin chips,

▲ LA CHATA

three-cheese salad and *tortilla de bacalao* (cod omelette).

Bars

Delic

Costanilla de San Andrés 14 ⓦ www
.deliccafe.com. Mon 8pm–2am, Tues–
Sat 11am–2am, Sun 11am–midnight.
Closed first half of Aug. Serving
home-made cakes, fruit juices
and coffee, this is a pleasant
café by day, transforming into a
crowded but friendly cocktail
bar by night. There's a good
summer *terraza* too.

María Panadora

Plaza Gabriel Miró 1. Tues–Thurs
7pm–2am, Fri & Sat 6pm–3am, Sun
4pm–2am. Closed second half of
Aug. An incongruous mix of
champagnería (champagne bar)
and library, where quality *cava*
can be enjoyed with the perfect
accompaniment of chocolates
and mellow jazz – a decadent
and highly enjoyable experience.

El Tempranillo

C/Cava Baja 38. Daily 1–4pm &
8pm–1am. Closed two weeks in Aug.
Popular little wine bar serving
a vast range of domestic wines
by the glass. A great place
to discover your favourite
Spanish *vino* – and the tapas are
excellent too.

El Ventorrillo

C/Bailén 14. Daily 11am–1am (till 2am
Fri & Sat). This popular *terraza*
is good for a relaxing drink
while enjoying the *vistillas*
(little views) over the Almudena
cathedral and the Guadarrama
mountains.

El Viajero

Plaza de la Cebada 11. Tues–Sat
1pm–2.30am, Sun 1–4.30pm.

Closed first half Jan, second half
Aug. Bar, club, restaurant and
summer *terraza* all in one, spread
over different floors of this
fashionable La Latina nightspot.
The food (meat, pizza and pasta)
is reasonable but it's best to stick
to a drink.

Flamenco tablaos

Las Carboneras

Plaza Conde de Miranda ☎ 915 428
677 ⓦ www.tablaolascarboneras
.com. Open Mon–Sat, shows 9pm
& 10.30pm (half an hour later at
weekends). A relative newcomer
to the restaurant/*tablao* scene,
geared to the tourist market and
slightly cheaper than its rivals,
but a very good alternative
if you want to get a taste of
flamenco.

Corral de la Morería

C/Morería 17 ☎ 913 658 446, ⓦ www
.corraldelamoreria.com. Mon–Thurs
8.30pm–2am, Fri & Sat till 2.30am.
A good, if expensive, venue
for serious flamenco acts,
where it's worth staying until
late in case there are any
spontaneous contributions from
the audience. Around €30 to
see the show and over double
that if you want to dine in the
restaurant as well.

La Soleá

C/Cava Baja 34 ☎ 913 653 308.
Mon–Sat 8.30pm–3am. Closed Aug.
This long-established flamenco
bar is the genuine article. People
sit around in the tiny salon, pick
up a guitar or start to sing and
gradually the atmosphere builds.
It does not have the sort of full-
scale show on offer in the two
venues mentioned above, but
the music and singing can be
astonishing.

The Palacio Real and Ópera

Although the barrio only became fashionable in the mid-nineteenth century, the attractions found in the compact area around Ópera metro station date back as far as the 1500s. The imposing and suitably lavish Palacio Real (Royal Palace) dominates this part of the city, bordered by the somewhat disappointing Catedral de la Almudena and the tranquil gardens of the Campo del Moro. The restored Teatro Real and Plaza de Oriente have brought back some nineteenth-century sophistication to the area, while the two monastery complexes of La Encarnación and Las Descalzas Reales conceal an astounding selection of artistic delights. For after-dark attractions, two of the city's leading clubs and a handful of pleasant cafés and restaurants are also nearby.

The Palacio Real

C/Bailén ⓦ www.patrimonionacional .es. April–Sept Mon–Sat 9am–6pm, Sun & hols 9am–3pm; Oct–March Mon–Sat 9.30am–5pm, Sun 9am–2pm; closed for state occasions. Tours €9, unguided €8, Wed free for EU citizens. The present Palacio Real (Royal Palace) was built by Felipe V after the ninth-century Arab-built Alcázar was destroyed in a fire in 1734. The Bourbon monarch, who had been brought up in the considerably more luxurious surroundings of Versailles, took the opportunity to replace it with an altogether grander affair. He did not, however, live to see its completion and the palace only became habitable in 1764 during the reign of Carlos III. Nowadays it's used only for ceremonial purposes, with the present royal family preferring the more modest Zarzuela Palace, 15 kilometres northwest of the city.

The ostentation lacking in the palace's exterior is more than compensated for inside, with swirling marble floors,

▼ PALACIO REAL INTERIOR

celestial frescoes, and gold furnishings filling the rooms. It's a flamboyant display of wealth and power that was firmly at odds with Spain's declining status at the time. Look out for the grandiose Salón del Trono (Throne Room), the incredible oriental-style Salón de Gasparini (the Gasparini Room) and the marvellous Sala de Porcelana (Porcelain Room), decorated with one thousand gold, green and white interlocking pieces.

The palace outbuildings and annexes include the recently refurbished **Armería Real** (Royal Armoury; separate ticket available if you're not visiting the rest of the palace €3.40), full of guns, swords and armour, with such curiosities as the suit of armour worn by Carlos V in his equestrian portrait by Titian in the Prado. Especially fascinating are the complete sets of armour designed for children, horses and dogs.

There's also an eighteenth-century **farmacia** (pharmacy), a mixture of scientific equipment and eccentric curiositites, whose walls are lined with jars labelled for various remedies, and a new **Galería de Pinturas** (an extra euro on the guided visit entry fee) with selected works by Caravaggio, Velázquez and Goya.

Jardines de Sabatini

Daily: April–Sept 9am–10pm; Oct–March 9am–9pm. The Jardines de Sabatini (Sabatini Gardens) make an ideal place from which to view the northern facade of the palace or to watch the sun go down. They contain an ornamental lake, some fragrant magnolia trees and well-manicured hedges, and, in summer, they're often used as a concert venue.

▲ CATEDRAL DE LA ALMUDENA

Catedral de la Almudena

Daily: summer 10am–2pm & 5–9pm; winter 9am–9pm. Not open for visits during mass: Mon–Sat 10am, noon, 6pm & 7pm, Sun & hols 10.30am, noon, 1.30pm, 6pm & 7pm. Free. Planned centuries ago, Madrid's cathedral, Nuestra Señora de la Almudena, was plagued by lack of funds, bombed out in the Civil War and eventually opened for business only in 1993. More recently it was the 2004 venue for the wedding of the heir to the throne, Prince Felipe, and his former newsreader bride, Letizia Ortiz.

Its stark, bulky Neoclassical facade was designed to match the Palacio Real opposite, while its cold Gothic interior is largely uninspiring. Exceptions include the brightly coloured ceiling designs, the sixteenth-century altarpiece in the Almudena chapel and a boutique-like chapel dedicated to José María Escrivá de Balaguer, the founder of the controversial Opus Dei religious movement in Madrid. The **crypt** (daily 10am–8pm; entrance on Cuesta de la Vega)

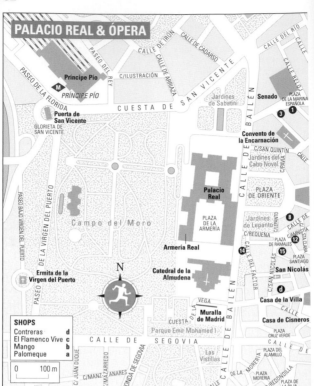

PALACIO REAL & ÓPERA

SHOPS

Contreras	d
El Flamenco Vive	c
Mango	b
Palomeque	a

0   100 m

with its forest of columns and dimly lit chapels is far more atmospheric than the main building.

El Campo del Moro

Entrance on Paseo de la Virgen del Puerto. April–Sept Mon–Sat

▼ ENTRANCE TO CAMPO DEL MORO

10am–8pm, Sun 9am–8pm; Oct–March Mon–Sat 10am–6pm, Sun 9am–6pm; closes occasionally for state occasions.

One of the most underused and beautiful of Madrid's parks, the Campo del Moro gets its name from being the site of the Moors' encampment, from where, in 1109, they mounted their unsuccessful attempt to reconquer Madrid. It later became a venue for medieval tournaments and celebrations. After the building of the Palacio Real several schemes to landscape the area were put forward, but

EATING, DRINKING & NIGHTLIFE

Al Norte	15	Caripén	3
El Anciano Rey		Casa Gallega	9 & 16
de los Vinos	14	Chocolatería San Ginés	13
La Bola	4	Entre Suspiro y Suspiro	7
El Buey	1	Joy Madrid	10
Café de Chinitas	2	Mushashi	5
Café de Oriente	8	Palacio de Gaviria	11
Café los Austrias	12	La Viuda Blanca	6

it wasn't until 1842 that things got under way. Based around two monumental fountains, *Las Conchas* and *Los Tritones*, the grassy gardens are very English in style, featuring shady paths and ornamental pools, and provide an excellent refuge from the summer heat, as well as a splendid view of the palace.

Plaza de Oriente

The aristocratic, pedestrianized Plaza de Oriente is one of the most attractive open spaces in Madrid. The days when Franco used to address crowds here from the balcony of the royal palace now seem a distant memory, although a small number of neo-Fascists still gather here on the anniversary of his death, November 21.

The showpiece fountain in the centre was designed by Narciso Pascual y Colomer, who also transferred the bronze equestrian statue of Felipe IV here from the garden of the Buen Retiro Palace, near the Prado. This statue is reputedly the first-ever bronze featuring a rearing horse – Galileo is said to have helped with the calculations to make it balance. Other statues depict Spanish kings and queens, and were originally designed to adorn the palace facade, but were too heavy or, according to one

▲ PLAZA DE ORIENTE

version, too ugly, and were removed on the orders of Queen Isabel of Farnese.

There's a very French feel to the buildings overlooking the square, with their glass-fronted balconies, underlined by the elegant neo-Baroque *Café de Oriente*, a favourite with the opera crowd.

Teatro Real

Plaza de Isabel II ☎915 160 660, box office ☎915 160 606, ticket line ☎902 244 848, ⓦwww.teatro-real .com. Open for visits Mon & Wed–Fri 10am–1.30pm, Sat, Sun & hols 11am–1.30pm; reservations ☎915 160 696. €4, tickets on sale 10am–1pm at the box office. When it opened in 1850, the hulking grey hexagonal opera house became the hub of fashionable Madrid and staged highly successful works by Verdi and Wagner. It fell into decay in the late twentieth century and after a ten-year refurbishment – that should have lasted four – and a staggering US$150 million in costs, it finally reopened in October 1997. With its lavish red and gold decor, crystal chandeliers, state-of-the-art lighting and superb acoustics it makes a truly magnificent setting for opera, ballet and classical concerts. Tickets range from €16 to €200, but you'll need to book well in advance for the best seats.

Convento de la Encarnación

Plaza de la Encarnación 1 ⓦwww .patrimonionacional.es. Tours only (some in English) Tues–Thurs & Sat 10.30am–12.45pm & 4–5.45pm, Fri 10.30am–12.45pm, Sun & hols 11am–1.45pm. €3.60; joint ticket with Monasterio de las Descalzas Reales €6, valid for a week; Wed free for EU citizens. Founded in 1611 by Felipe III and his wife Margarita de Austria, this convent was intended as a retreat for titled women and merits a visit for its reliquary alone – one of the most important in the Catholic world. The solemn granite facade is the hallmark of architect Juan Gómez de Mora, also responsible for the Plaza Mayor. Much of the painting contained within is uninspiring, but there are some interesting items, including an extensive collection of royal portraits and a highly prized collection of sculptures of Christ. The library-like reliquary contains more than 1500 saintly relics from around the world: skulls, arms encased in beautifully ornate hand-shaped containers, and bones from every conceivable part of the body. The most famous of the lot is a small glass bulb said to contain the blood of St Pantaleón – a fourteenth-century doctor martyr – which supposedly liquefies at midnight on the eve of his feast day (July 26). The tour ends with a visit to the Baroque-style church which features a beautifully frescoed ceiling and a marble-columned altarpiece.

Monasterio de las Descalzas Reales

Plaza de las Descalzas 3 ⓦ www
.patrimonionacional.es. Tours only
(some in English) Tues–Thurs & Sat
10.30am–12.45pm & 4–5.45pm,
Fri 10.30am–12.45pm, Sun & hols
11am–1.45pm. €5; joint ticket with
Convento de la Encarnación €6,
valid for a week; Wed free for EU
citizens. One of the less well
known treasures of Madrid, the
"Monastery of the Barefoot
Royal Ladies" was originally the
site of a medieval palace. The
building was transformed by
Juana de Austria into a convent
in 1564, and the architect of El
Escorial, Juan Bautista de Toledo,
was entrusted with its design.
Juana was the youngest daughter
of the Emperor Carlos V and,
at the age of 19, already the
widow of Prince Don Juan of
Portugal. Royal approval meant
that it soon became home to a
succession of titled ladies who
brought with them an array
of artistic treasures, helping
the convent accumulate a
fabulous collection of paintings,
sculptures and tapestries. The
place is still unbelievably

opulent and remains in use as a religious institution, housing 23 shoeless nuns of the Franciscan order.

The magnificent main staircase connects a two-levelled cloister, lined with small but richly embellished chapels, while the Tapestry Room contains an outstanding collection of early seventeenth-century Flemish tapestries based on designs by Rubens.

Iglesia San Ginés

C/Arenal 13. Mon 12.30pm. Free.
The recently restored church of San Ginés is of Mozarabic origin (built by Christians under Moorish rule) but its chief attraction is an outstanding El Greco canvas of the moneychangers being chased from the temple which he painted towards the end of his life in 1614 and is on show to the public on Mondays at 12.30pm.

▼ MONASTERIO DE LAS DESCALZAS REALES

Casa de las Alhajas

Plaza San Martín 1 ⓦwww
.fundacioncajamadrid.es. Tues–Sun
10am–8pm. Free. This three-
floored exhibition space, run
by local bank Caja Madrid,
hosts a range of interesting and
well-presented temporary shows
that are usually a cut above
many of the others in the city.
Recent highlights have included
exhibitions on Sorolla and
Picasso.

Shops

Contreras

C/Mayor 80 ⓦ www.manuelcontreras
.com. Mon–Fri 10am–1.30pm &
5–8pm, Sat 10am–1.30pm. Award-
winning guitar workshop, run
on this site for over 40 years by
the Contreras family, the perfect
place for budding flamenco
artists to buy the genuine article.

▼ CAFÉ DE ORIENTE

El Flamenco Vive

C/Conde de Lemos 7 ⓦwww
.elflamencovive.es. Mon–Sat 10.30am–
2pm & 5–9pm. A fascinating little
slice of Andalucía in Madrid,
specializing in all things
flamenco, from guitars and CDs
to dresses and books.

Mango

C/Arenal 24 ⓦ www.mango.es.
Mon–Sat 10am–9pm. A central
branch of one of Spain's most
popular chain stores for young
women. A wide range of smart
and casual wear that won't break
the bank.

Palomeque

C/Hileras 12. Mon–Fri 9.30am–1.30pm
& 4.30–8pm, Sat 9.30am–1.30pm. A
religious department store and
the place to come if you want to
complete your postcard collection
of Spanish saints and virgins.

Cafés

Café los Austrias

Plaza de Ramales 1.
Mon–Thurs 9am–1.30am,
Fri–Sat 9am–2.30am,
Sun 9am–midnight.
Relaxing old-
fashioned café, with
marble table-tops and
dark-wood interior.
Service is slow but
it makes a good stop
after a visit to the
Palacio Real.

Café de Oriente

Plaza de Oriente 2.
Mon–Thurs & Sun
8.30am–1.30am, Fri &
Sat till 2.30am. Elegant,
Parisian-style café
with a popular
terraza looking
across the plaza to
the palace. The café

– which also houses a prestigious restaurant – was opened in the 1980s by a priest, Padre Lezama, who ploughs his profits into various charitable schemes. There's an equally smart bar, *La Botilleria* (open noon–1am, an hour later on Fri & Sat), next door.

▲ CASA GALLEGA

Chocolatería San Ginés

Pasadizo de San Ginés 11. Daily 9.30am–7am. A Madrid institution, this café, established in 1894, serves *chocolate con churros* (thick hot chocolate with deep-fried hoops of batter) to perfection – just the thing to finish off a night of excess. It's an almost compulsory Madrileño custom to end up here after the clubs close, before heading home for a shower and then off to work.

Restaurants

Al Norte

C/San Nicólas 8 ☎ 915 472 222, ⊛ www.alnorte.es. Mon–Sat 1.30–4pm & 8.45pm–midnight, Sun 1.30–4pm. As the name would suggest, this stylish restaurant, which is nestled in an atmospheric back street close to the Palacio Real, specializes in produce from the north of Spain. It does a fine €15 *menú del día* at lunch time as well as a variety of other menu options (ranging €35–€55) in the evening. Traditional dishes served with a creative twist.

La Bola

C/Bola 5 ☎ 915 476 930, ⊛ www .labola.es. Mon–Sat 1–4pm & 8.30–11.30pm, Sun 1–4pm. Opened back in 1870, this is the place to go for *cocido madrileño* (soup followed by chickpeas and a selection of meats) cooked in the traditional way over a wood fire (lunch times only for €19). Try the delicious *buñuelos de manzana* (battered apples) for pudding, and don't plan on doing anything energetic afterwards. They don't accept cards.

El Buey

Plaza de la Marina Española 1 ☎ 915 413 041. Mon–Sat 1–4pm & 9pm–midnight. A meat-eaters' paradise, specializing in superb steak that you fry yourself on a hotplate. Great side dishes and home-made desserts, with a highly drinkable house red, all for around €35 per head.

Caripén

Plaza Marina Española 4 ☎ 915 411 177. Mon–Sat 9pm–3am. Closed Aug. Quality French restaurant with excellent *magret de pato* (duck) and very tasty sauces. Open until the early hours, but its popularity with Spanish celebrities means it's overpriced and service can be patchy. Expect to pay around €40 a head.

Casa Gallega

C/Bordadores 11 ☎ 915 419 055; also Plaza San Miguel 8 ☎ 915 473 055. Daily 1–4pm & 8pm–midnight. Two airy and welcoming *marisquerías* that have been importing seafood on overnight trains from Galicia since opening in 1915. Costs vary according to the market price of the fish or shellfish that you order. *Pulpo* (octopus) and *pimientos de Padrón* (small peppers, spiced up by the odd fiery one) are brilliantly done and inexpensive, but the more exotic seasonal delights will raise a bill to around €40 a head.

Entre Suspiro y Suspiro

C/Caños de Peral 3 ☎915 420 644. Mon–Fri 2–4.30pm & 9.30–11.30pm, Sat 9.30–11.30pm. Given Madrid's links with Latin America, this is one of surprisingly few decent Mexican restaurants in the city. Quesadillas, tacos and fajitas served up in pleasant surroundings, although it is rather cramped and prices are high at around €40 for a meal.

Mushashi

C/Conchas 4 ☎915 592 939. Tues–Sun 1.30–4pm & 8.30–11.30pm. The best-value Japanese restaurant in town. The sushi, sashimi and tempura are all excellent, service is friendly and prices reasonable.

La Viuda Blanca

C/Campomanes 6 ☎915 487 529 ☻www.laviudablanca.com. Mon–Sat 1–5pm & 9pm–1am. A self-consciously super-cool restaurant with the de rigeur minimalist decor, serving an inventive €12 set lunch (€15 at the weekends) with vegetarian and low-calorie options. On the other side of the bar is *La Viuda Negra* club/cocktail bar.

Bars

El Anciano Rey de los Vinos

C/Bailén 19. Mon, Tues & Thurs–Sun 10am–3pm & 6–11pm. Traditional standing-room-only bar founded back in 1909, serving well-poured beer, a decent selection of wine and some good standard tapas.

Discobares and clubs

Joy Madrid

C/Arenal 11 ☻www.joy-eslava .com. Daily 11.30pm–6am. €12–15 including first drink. This big-name

▼ JOY MADRID CLUB

club is home to the thirty-something crowd rather than serious clubbers and is frequented by musicians, models, media folk and footballers. Long queues and a strict door policy, so dress smart to increase your chances of getting in. If you can't, console yourself at the nearby *Chocolatería San Ginés* (see p.67).

Palacio de Gaviria

C/Arenal 9 ⓦwww.palaciogaviria.com. Daily 11pm–late. €10–15 including drink. Nineteenth-century palace with a series of extravagant Baroque salons playing anything from house to tropical (a genre taking in everything from salsa to rumba). A fantastic setting for a late drink, it hosts occasional "International Parties" (a common term here for parties aimed at students of different nationalities studying in Madrid) and dance classes too.

Live music

Café de Chinitas

C/Torija 7 ☏915 595 135, ⓦwww .chinitas.com. Mon–Thurs 9pm–2am, Fri & Sat 9pm–3am. Drinks and show €32. One of the oldest flamenco clubs in Madrid, hosting a dinner-dance spectacular. The music is authentic but keep an eye on how much you order as the bill can soon mount up. Reservations essential.

The Rastro, Lavapiés and Embajadores

Lavapiés and Embajadores were originally tough, working-class districts built to accommodate the huge population growth of the eighteenth and nineteenth centuries. Traditional sights are thin on the ground, but some original tenement blocks survive and the city's former industrial and commercial centre is now famous for the Rastro street market. These barrios are also home to the *castizos* – authentic Madrileños – who can be seen decked out in traditional costume during local festivals. The character of these areas has changed, however, in recent years. Young, trendy Spaniards and large numbers of immigrants have arrived, meaning that Lavapiés and Embajadores are now Madrid's most racially mixed barrios, with teahouses, kebab joints and textile shops sitting alongside some of the most original bars and restaurants in the city. Petty crime can be a problem round here but the reality is not as dramatic as newspapers suggest.

Iglesia-Catedral de San Isidro

C/Toledo 37. Mon–Sat 7.45am–1pm & 6–8.45pm, Sun & hols 8.30am–2pm & 6–8.30pm. Built from 1622 to 1633, this enormous twin-towered church was originally the centre of the Jesuit Order in Spain. After Carlos III fell out with the Order in 1767, he redesigned the interior and dedicated it to the city's patron, San Isidro. Isidro's remains – and those of his equally saintly wife – were brought here in 1769 from the nearby Iglesia de San Andrés (see p.54).

The church was the city's provisional cathedral from 1886 until 1993 when the new Catedral de la Almudena (see p.61) was finally completed. It contains a single nave with large, ornate lateral chapels and an impressive altarpiece.

El Rastro

Every Sunday morning the heaving, ramshackle mass of El Rastro flea market takes over Calle Ribera de Curtidores. On

▲ GOODS ON SALE AT EL RASTRO FLEA MARKET

offer is just about anything you might – or more likely might not – need, from second-hand clothes and military surplus items to caged birds and fine antiques.

The area was formerly the site of two large slaughterhouses and the resulting blood that flowed down the hill gave it its name (*rastro* means stain). The establishment of the slaughterhouses acted as a magnet for other traders and craftsmen: tanners – *curtidores*, hence the street name – and food sellers all soon set up here.

Real bargains are few and far between, but the atmosphere is always enjoyable and the bars around these streets are as good as any in the city. Be aware though, that petty theft is a big problem here, so keep a close eye on your belongings.

Puerta de Toledo

One of several monumental gates that ring the city centre, Puerta de Toledo stands as an eloquent testament to the political vicissitudes of nineteenth-century Madrid. Originally commissioned by Joseph Bonaparte to commemorate his accession to the Spanish throne, the arch ended up being a celebration of his defeat when it was completed in 1827.

Alongside, the **Mercado Puerta de Toledo** was once the site of the city's fish market and now has pretensions to being a stylish arts, crafts and antiques centre though it is still trying to attract business.

Estadio Vicente Calderón

Paseo Virgen del Puerto 67 ☎ 913 664 707, ⊛ www.clubatleticodemadrid .com. Match tickets start at around €30. Ticket hotline ☎ 902 530 530 and available via the website. Home

to Atlético Madrid, one of the city's two big-name football teams, this 54,000-capacity stadium makes for quite a sight as its smoked-glass sides rise high above the Manzanares river and the newly reformed subterranean M30 ring road. Atlético may not have tasted the glory experienced by rivals Real Madrid, but the club still ranks as one of Spain's biggest teams and the Calderón is packed with loyal fans for weekend league matches. The stadium also houses a decent **club shop** (Mon–Fri 10am–2pm & 2–8pm, Sat & Sun 10am–2pm, match days 11am–45 mins before kickoff) and a **museum** (Tues–Sun 11am–7pm; €6, guided tours an extra €2) detailing the history and achievements of one of the country's best supported teams.

La Corrala

C/Tribulete 12 ☎ 915 309 600.
Built in 1839 and restored in the 1980s, this is one of many traditional *corrales* (tenement blocks) in Lavapiés, with balconied apartments opening onto a central patio. Plays, especially farces and *zarzuelas* (a mix of classical opera and music-hall bawdiness), used to be performed regularly in Spanish *corrales*, and the open space adjacent to the neighbouring church usually hosts performances in the

▼ LA CORRALA HOUSING BLOCK

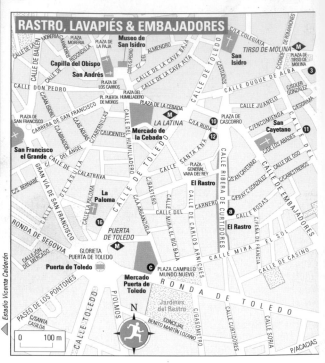

RASTRO, LAVAPIÉS & EMBAJADORES

▲ Estadio Vicente Calderón

summer as part of the *Veranos de la Villa* cultural programme (see Essentials, p.178).

San Cayetano

C/Embajadores 15. Variable hours, usually Mon–Sat 9.30am–12pm & 6–8pm, Sun 9am–2pm & 6–8pm.
This remarkable Baroque-style church is dedicated to the patron saint of one of the area's most important festivals (see p.179). José de Churriguera and Pedro de Ribera, both renowned for their extravagant designs, were involved in the design of the elaborately sculpted facade, which dates from 1761. Most of the rest of the church was destroyed in the Civil War and has since been rebuilt.

Plaza Lavapiés

In the Middle Ages, bustling Plaza Lavapiés was the core of Jewish Madrid, with the synagogue situated on the southern side of the square.

▲ PLAZA LAVAPIÉS METRO

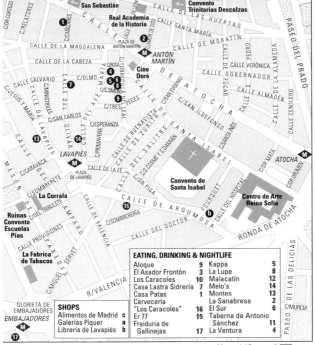

EATING, DRINKING & NIGHTLIFE

Aloque	9	Kappa	5
El Asador Frontón	3	La Lupe	8
Los Caracoles	10	Malacatín	12
Casa Lastra Sidrería	7	Melo's	14
Casa Patas	1	Montes	13
Cervecería		La Sanabresa	2
"Los Caracoles"	16	El Sur	6
Er 77	15	Taberna de Antonio	
Freiduria de		Sánchez	11
Gallinejas	17	La Ventura	4

SHOPS

Alimentos de Madrid	c
Galerías Piquer	a
Librería de Lavapiés	b

Museo del Ferrocarril ▽

Today, with its Chinese, Arabic and African inhabitants, it remains a cosmopolitan place, and the plaza, along with the c/Argumosa running off from its southeastern corner, is an animated spot, with a variety of bars and cafés in various states of decay.

Calle Atocha

Calle Atocha, one of the old ceremonial routes from Plaza Mayor to the basilica at Atocha, forms the northeastern border of Lavapiés. At its southern end it's a mishmash of fast-food and touristy restaurants, developing, as you move north up the hill, into a strange mixture of cheap hostels, fading shops, bars, lottery kiosks and sex emporia.

With its brash neon lighting and shiny black facade, the huge sex shop at no. 80, El Mundo Fantástico, stands unashamedly opposite a convent and the site of an old printing house that produced the first edition of the first part of *Don Quixote*.

Cine Doré

C/Santa Isabel 3 ☎914 672 600. Closed Mon. Films €2.50. At the end of the narrow Pasaje Doré alley is the Cine Doré, the oldest cinema in Madrid. Dating from 1922 with a later *Modernista*/Art Nouveau facade, it's now the Filmoteca Nacional, an art-house cinema with bargain prices and a pleasant, inexpensive café/restaurant (Tues–Sun 1.30pm–12.30am).

▲ CINE DORÉ

Museo del Ferrocarril

Paseo de las Delicias 61 ☎ 902 228 822, ⓦ www.museodelferrocarril.org. Tues–Sun 10am–3pm. Closed Aug. €4. The Museo del Ferrocarril (railway museum) contains an impressive assortment of engines, carriages and wagons that once graced the train lines of Spain. The museum, which is housed in the handsome old station of Delicias, also has a fascinating collection of model railways and there's an atmospheric little café in one of the more elegant carriages.

Shops

Alimentos de Madrid

Mercado de Toledo, 2nd floor ⓦ www .alimentosdemadrid.org. Mon–Sat 10.30am–2pm & 5–8.30pm, Sun 10.30am–2pm. Financed by the local authority, this outlet in the Mercado de Toledo shopping centre showcases a wide variety of regional produce including wine, olive oil and honey.

Galerías Piquer

C/Ribera de Curtidores 29. Mon–Fri 10.30am–2pm & 5–8pm, Sat & Sun 10.30am–2pm. Rather more upmarket than the nearby Rastro flea market, this arcade contains a wide selection of interesting antique shops.

Librería de Lavapiés

C/Argumosa 39 ⓦ www .lalibreriadelavapies.com. Mon–Sat 10am–10pm, Sun 11am–9pm. Friendly local bookshop selling a carefully chosen selection of Spanish fiction and poetry. It also has a small section of second-hand English books for children and adults tucked away at the back.

Cafés

Nuevo Café Barbieri

C/Avemaría 45. Daily 3pm–2am, Fri & Sat till 3am. A relaxed, slightly dilapidated café, with unobtrusive music, lots of wooden tables, old-style decor, newspapers and a wide selection of coffees.

Restaurants

El Asador Frontón

Plaza Tirso de Molina 7, 1º (entrance on c/Jesus y María) ☎ 913 691 617. Mon–Sat 1–4pm & 9pm–midnight, Sun 1–4pm. Charming, old neighbourhood restaurant where locals come for a long lunch. There's a range of delicious Castilian dishes and some fine home-made desserts. Expect to pay around €40 for the works.

Casa Lastra Sidrería

C/Olivar 3 ☎ 913 691 482, ⓦ www .casalastra.com. Mon, Tues & Thurs–Sat 1–5pm & 8pm–midnight, Sun 1–5pm. Closed July. Very popular and moderately priced restaurant serving classic Asturian fare: *chorizo a la sidra* (chorizo in cider), *entrecot al cabrales* (steak in a strong blue-cheese sauce), *fabada* (a warming winter stew of beans, *chorizo* and black pudding) and, of course, *sidra natural* (cider). Big portions and at €12.50 the set lunch is very good value.

Malacatín

C/Ruda 5 ☎913 655 241, ⓦwww .malacatin.com. Mon–Fri 1–4pm & 8–11pm, Sat 1–5pm. Closed Aug. Established in 1893 to serve wine to local workmen, this authentic *castizo* restaurant serves up generous helpings of what is arguably the best *cocido* in the city for a reasonable €18. You can sample it at the bar for €5 too if you haven't the appetite for the full monty.

La Sanabresa

C/Amor de Diós 12 ☎914 290 338. Mon–Sat 1–4pm & 8.30–11.30pm, Fri & Sat till midnight. Closed Aug. Down-to-earth local restaurant with an endless supply of customers coming for its excellent and reasonably priced dishes. There are two *menús del día* for €8–9 and dinner is equally good value. Friendly staff give plenty of advice. Don't miss the grilled aubergines.

Tapas bars

Los Caracoles

Plaza Cascorro 18. Mon–Thurs 11am–4pm, Fri & Sat 11am–4pm & 7–10.30pm, Sun 10am–4pm. A favourite since the 1940s, this classic bar does a good range of tapas including the eponymous *caracoles* (snails). On Sundays it's always heaving with customers who have worked up an

appetite browsing the Rastro.

Cervecería "Los Caracoles"

C/Toledo 106. Tues–Sat 9am–10.30pm, Sun 9am–4pm. Closed July. Another place specializing in snails. A continual supply is served up in a wonderful spicy sauce in this rough-and-ready local bar, all washed down with the local *vermút del grifo* (draught vermouth).

Er 77

C/Argumosa 8. Daily 1–5pm & 8.30pm–midnight. A small, very popular bar situated in the middle of this pleasant tree-lined street running off Plaza Lavapiés. Excellent *raciones*, inventive salads, friendly service and good wines.

Freiduría de Gallinejas

C/Embajadores 84. Mon–Sat 11am–11pm. Closed Aug. This traditional tiled, family-run bar is famed for serving the best fried lambs' intestines in the city. A variety of different cuts of this very popular local dish are available as well as straightforward fried lamb. Not to everyone's taste though.

Melo's

C/Avemaría 44. Tues–Sat 9am–2am. Closed Aug. Standing room only at this very popular Galician bar serving huge *zapatillas* (hunks of bread filled with *lacón* – shoulder of pork – and cheese) plus great *pimientos de Padrón* and some fine *croquetas*.

El Sur

C/Torrecilla del Leal 12. Tues–Thurs 8pm–midnight, Fri–Sun 2–4.30pm & 8pm–1am. Imaginative and good-value tapas in a friendly bar decked out in posters from famous Spanish films. Popular options are the *ropa vieja* (a Cuban dish made with cuts of beef) and the moussaka. A fine selection of wines too.

Taberna de Antonio Sánchez

C/Mesón de Paredes 13. Mon–Sat noon–4pm & 8pm–midnight, Sun noon–4pm. Said to be the oldest *taberna* in Madrid, this seventeenth-century bar has a stuffed bull's head (to commemorate Antonio Sánchez, the son of the founder, who was killed by a bull) and a wooden interior. Lots of *finos* on offer, plus *jamón* and *queso* tapas or *tortilla de San Isidro* (omelette with salted cod).

▲ CASA PATAS RESTAURANT

Bars

Aloque

C/Torrecilla del Leal 20. Daily 7.30pm–1am. Closed Aug. Relaxed wine bar where you can try top-quality *vinos* by the glass. The tapas, served up from the tiny kitchen at the back, are original and extremely good.

Montes

C/Lavapiés 40. Tues–Sat noon–4pm & 7.30pm–midnight, Sun 11am–3.30pm. Closed Aug. A Lavapiés favourite for those in search of a decent glass of wine and a very tasty canapé. Ask owner César for advice and he'll help find the best ones for you. A great place to start the evening.

Discobares and clubs

Kappa

C/Olmo 26. Tues–Thurs & Sun 8.30pm–2am, Fri & Sat 8.30pm–3.30am.

Relaxing chill-out bar, with comfy seats, good music and a mixed gay and straight crowd. DJs get the party started at the weekend.

La Lupe

C/Torrecilla del Leal 12. Daily 9pm–2.30am. Mixed gay, lesbian and alternative bar with good music, cheap drinks and occasional cabaret.

La Ventura

C/Olmo 31.Wed 11pm–2am, Fri & Sat 11pm–2.30am, Sun 8pm–2am. It's easy to walk by the unobtrusive entrance, but this three-floored club is one of the mainstays of the Lavapiés nightscene. Trip hop, dub and drum 'n' bass from top-notch DJs.

Flamenco tablaos

Casa Patas

C/Cañizares 10 ☎913 690 496, ⓦwww.casapatas.com. Shows Mon–Thurs 10.30pm, Fri & Sat 9pm & midnight. €27. Authentic flamenco club with a bar and restaurant that gets its share of big names. The best nights are Thursday and Friday – check the website for schedules.

Sol, Santa Ana and Huertas

The busy transport and shopping hub of Puerta del Sol and the streets around Plaza Santa Ana and Huertas are the bustling heart of Madrid and the reference point for most visitors to the capital. The city began to expand here during the sixteenth century and the area subsequently became known as the *barrio de las letras* (literary neighbourhood) because of the many authors and playwrights – including Cervantes – who made it their home. Today, the literary theme continues, with theatres, bookshops and cafés proliferating alongside the Ateneo (literary, scientific and political club), the Círculo de Bellas Artes (Fine Arts Institute), the Teatro Español (historic theatre specializing in classic works) and the Congreso de Los Diputados (Parliament). For art lovers, there's the Real Academia de Bellas Artes de San Fernando, an important museum and gallery. For most visitors, though, the main attraction is the vast array of traditional bars, particularly concentrated around the picturesque Plaza Santa Ana.

Puerta del Sol

This half-moon-shaped plaza, thronged with people and traffic at almost any hour of the day, marks the centre of the city and, indeed, of Spain – **Kilometre Zero**, an inconspicuous stone slab on the south side of the square, is the spot from which all distances in the country are measured. Opposite, near an equestrian bronze of King Carlos III, stands a statue of Madrid's emblem, **el oso y el madroño** (bear and strawberry tree).

▼ NEON TIO PEPE SIGN IN PUERTA DEL SOL

SOL, SANTA ANA & HUERTAS

The square has been a popular meeting place since the mid-sixteenth century, when it was the site of one of the main gates into the city. Its most important building is the **Casa de Correos**, built in 1766 and originally the city's post office. Under Franco it became the headquarters of the much-feared security police and now houses the main offices of the Madrid regional government. The Neoclassical facade is crowned by the nation's most famous clock which officially ushers in the New Year: on December 31, Madrileños pack Puerta del Sol and attempt to scoff twelve grapes – one on each of the chimes of midnight – to bring themselves good luck for the next twelve months.

The square has also witnessed several incidents of national importance, including the slaughter of a rioting crowd by Napoleon's marshal, Murat, aided by the infamous Egyptian cavalry, on May 2, 1808. The event is depicted in Goya's canvas, *Dos de Mayo*, now hanging in the Prado (see p.90). The area is likely to experience disruption of a very different sort over the next few years with the construction of a subterranean train station beneath c/Montera.

Plaza Santa Ana

The main reason for visiting vibrant Plaza Santa Ana is to explore the mass of bars, restaurants and cafés on the square itself and in the nearby streets that bring the area alive in the evenings.

The square was one of a series created by Joseph Bonaparte,

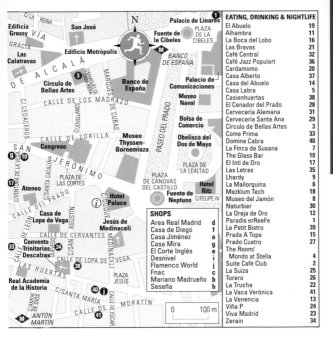

EATING, DRINKING & NIGHTLIFE	
El Abuelo	19
Alhambra	11
La Boca del Lobo	16
Las Bravas	21
Café Central	32
Café Jazz Populart	36
Cardamomo	20
Casa Alberto	37
Casa del Abuelo	14
Casa Labra	5
Casienhuertas	38
El Cenador del Prado	28
Cervecería Alemana	31
Cervecería Santa Ana	29
Círculo de Bellas Artes	3
Come Prima	33
Domine Cabra	40
La Finca de Susana	7
The Glass Bar	10
El Inti de Oro	17
Las Letras	35
Lhardy	9
La Mallorquina	6
Mezklum Tech	18
Museo del Jamón	8
Naturbier	30
La Oreja de Oro	12
Paradis erReeFe	1
Le Petit Bistro	39
Prada A Tope	15
Prado Cuatro	27
The Room/ Mondo at Stella	4
Suite Café Club	2
La Suiza	25
Torero	26
La Trucha	22
La Vaca Verónica	41
La Venencia	13
Viña P	24
Viva Madrid	23
Zerain	34

SHOPS	
Area Real Madrid	d
Casa de Diego	f
Casa Jiménez	a
Casa Mira	g
El Corte Inglés	e
Desnivel	i
Flamenco World	j
Fnac	c
Mariano Madrueño	b
Seseña	h

whose passion for open spaces led to a remarkable remodelling of Madrid in the six short years of his reign. It's dominated by two distinguished buildings at either end: to the west, the newly refurbished *ME Madrid*, a giant white confection of a hotel; to the east, the nineteenth-century Neoclassical **Teatro Español**. There has been a playhouse on this site since 1583, and the current theatre is the oldest in Madrid, its facade decorated with busts of famous Spanish playwrights.

Casa de Lope de Vega

C/Cervantes 11. Tues–Fri 9.30am–2pm, Sat 10am–1.30pm (knock if the door is closed). Closed mid-July to mid-Aug. €2, Sat free. Situated in the heart of the Huertas district, the reconstructed home of the great golden age Spanish dramatist offers a fascinating glimpse of life in seventeenth-century Madrid. Lope de Vega, a prolific

▼ CASA DE LOPE DE VEGA

writer with a tangled private life, lived here for 25 years until his death in 1635 at the age of 48. The house itself has been furnished in authentic fashion using the inventory left at the writer's death and highlights include a chapel containing some of his relics, his study with a selection of contemporary books, and a harem. The garden has been replanted and designed according to references found in the writer's correspondence.

Cervantes lived and died at no. 2 on the same street and though the original building has long gone, a plaque above a shop marks the site.

Ateneo Artístico, Científico y Literario

C/Prado 2. Mon–Sat 9am–12.45am, Sun & hols 9am–9.45pm. The Ateneo (literary, scientific and political club) was founded after the 1820 Revolution and provided a focus for the new liberal political ideas circulating at that time. The exterior is Neo-plateresque in style, while the inside features a Neoclassical lecture theatre, a wooden panelled corridor with portraits of past presidents of the club and a splendid reading room. It also has a good-value café.

El Congreso de los Diputados

Plaza de las Cortes ⓦ www.congreso .es. Sat 10.30am–1pm (bring passport). Closed Aug & hols. The lower house of the Spanish parliament meets in a rather unprepossessing nineteenth-century building. Its most distinguished feature is the two bronze lions that guard the entrance, made from a melted-down cannon captured during the African War of 1859–60.

Sessions can be visited by appointment only, though anyone can turn up and queue for a free tour on Saturday mornings. This takes in several of the most important rooms and the chamber itself where the bullet holes left by mad Colonel Tejero and his Guardia Civil associates in the abortive coup of 1981 are pointed out.

Calle Alcalá

An imposing catalogue of Spanish architecture lines Calle Alcalá, an ancient thoroughfare that originally led to the Roman university town of Alcalá de Henares. It starts at Puerta del Sol and in this first stretch look out particularly for the splendid early twentieth-century wedge-shaped Banco Español de Crédito adorned with elephant heads and plaques listing all the branches of the bank

▲ BANCO ESPAÑOL DE CRÉDITO

in Spain, soon to be turned into a luxury hotel, shopping centre and apartment block. The Banco de Bilbao Vizcaya, with its Neoclassical concave facade complete with charioteers on top; and the Baroque Ministerio de Hacienda (Inland Revenue) are similarly impressive.

Iglesia de San José

C/Alcalá 41. Daily 8am–1pm & 6–8pm, Sun open from 9am. The red-brick Iglesia de San José, near the junction with Gran Vía, dates back to the 1730s and was the last building designed by the prolific Pedro de Ribera. The interior holds the ornate Santa Teresa de Ávila chapel and an impressive collection of colourful images of Christ and the Virgin Mary.

Iglesia de Las Calatravas

C/Alcalá 25. Mon–Fri 8am–1pm & 6–8pm, Sat & Sun 11am–2pm & 6–8pm. Free. The pastel-pink Iglesia de Las Calatravas was built in the seventeenth century for the nuns of the Calatrava, one of the four Spanish military orders. Inside, it contains a fantastically elaborate gold altarpiece by José Churriguera.

Museo de la Real Academia de Bellas Artes de San Fernando

C/Alcalá 13 ☎915 240 864, ⊛rabasf .insde.es. Tues–Fri 9am–7pm, Sat 9am–2.30pm & 4–7pm, Mon, Sun & hols 9am–2.30pm. €3, free Wed. Established by Felipe V in 1744 and housed in its present location since 1773, the Museo de la Real Academia de Bellas Artes de San Fernando is one of the most important art galleries in Spain. Its displays include sections on sculpture, architecture and music, some interesting French and Italian

work, and an extraordinary – but chaotically displayed – collection of Spanish paintings, including El Greco, Velázquez, Murillo and Picasso.

The Goya section has two revealing self-portraits, several depictions of the despised royal favourite *Don Manuel Godoy*, the desolate representation of *The Madhouse*, and *The Burial of the Sardine* (a popular procession that continues to this day in Madrid).

The gallery is also home to the national chalcography collection (Mon–Fri 10am–2pm, Sat 10am–1.30pm; free), which includes some Goya etchings and several of the copper plates used for his *Capricho* series on show in the Prado.

Círculo de Bellas Artes

C/Marqués de Casa Riera 2. Exhibitions Tues–Fri 5–9pm, Sat 11am–2pm & 5–9pm, Sun 11am–2pm. €1. This striking 1920s Art Deco building, crowned by a statue of Pallas Athene, is home to one of Madrid's best arts centres. Inside there's a theatre, music hall, exhibition galleries, cinema and a very relaxing café bar (see p.87).

For many years a stronghold of Spain's intelligentsia, it attracts the city's arts and media crowd but is not exclusive, nor expensive. As the Círculo is theoretically a members-only club, it issues day membership on the door, for which you get access to all areas.

Plaza de la Cibeles

Encircled by four of the most monumental buildings in Madrid – the Palacio de Comunicaciones (the Post Office), Banco de España (the Central Bank), the Palacio de Buenavista (the Army HQ)

▲ STATUE OF THE GODDESS CIBELES IN PLAZA DE LA CIBELES

each province, while the interior preserves a totally Byzantine system, with scores of counters each offering a particular service, from telegrams to string. The building has been usurped by the over-mighty Madrid city council and will eventually provide a home for the burgeoning municipal offices.

Palacio de Linares

Plaza de la Cibeles 2 ⓦ www.casamerica.es. Tues–Sat 11am–7pm, Sun 11am–2pm. This palatial eighteenth-century mansion, built by the Marqués de Linares, is now home to the Casa de América, a cultural organization that promotes Latin American art through an ambitious programme of concerts, films and exhibitions. It also has a good bookshop, a fine restaurant (see p.85) and an excellent summer garden terrace.

and the Palacio de Linares (the Casa de América) – Plaza de la Cibeles is one of the city's most famous landmarks. At its centre, and marooned in a sea of never-ending traffic, is the late eighteenth-century fountain and statue of the goddess Cibeles, riding in a chariot drawn by two lions. Built to celebrate the city's first public water supply, today the fountain sees celebrations of a different kind as the favoured location for Real Madrid fans to congregate after a victory (Atlético supporters bathe in the fountain of Neptune just down the road).

Palacio de Comunicaciones

This grandiose wedding-cake of a building, constructed between 1904 and 1917, is Madrid's main post office. Much more imposing than the parliament, the exterior is flanked by polished brass postboxes for

Shops

Area Real Madrid

C/Carmen 3. Mon–Sat 10am–9pm, Sun 11am–8pm. Club store where you can pick up replica shirts and all manner of – expensive – souvenirs related to the club's history. There is another branch in the shopping centre on the corner of Real's Bernabéu stadium at c/Concha Espina 1.

Casa de Diego

Puerta del Sol 12 ⓦ www.casadediego .net. Mon–Sat 9.30am–8pm. Old-fashioned shop with helpful staff selling a fabulous array of

Spanish fans (*abanicos*) ranging from cheap offerings at under €5 to beautifully hand-crafted works of art costing up to €200. Sells umbrellas, walking sticks and shawls too.

Casa Jiménez

C/Preciados 42. Mon–Sat 10am–1.30pm & 5–8pm, closed Sat pm in July and all day Sat in Aug. One of the oldest shops in Spain, where you can buy elaborately embroidered *mantones* (shawls) made in Seville, with prices from €100 to €600, as well as gorgeous fans from around €40.

Casa Mira

Carrera de San Jerónimo 30. Daily 10am–2pm & 5–9pm. The place to go for *turrón* (flavoured nougat, eaten by nearly all Spaniards at Christmas) and marzipan. The family business has been open for over a hundred and fifty years since the founder, Luis Mira, arrived from Asturias and set up a stall in Puerta del Sol.

El Corte Inglés

C/Preciados 1–4. Mon–Sat 10am–9pm & first Sun in the month. The Spanish department store *par excellence*. It's not cheap, but the quality is very good, plus the staff are highly professional (the majority speak English) and there's an upmarket food department too.

Desnivel

Plaza Matute 6 ⊛www.libreriadesnivel.com. Mon–Sat 10am–2pm & 4.30–8.30pm. The place to come for maps and guides if you fancy a hike in the nearby Sierra Guadarrama.

Flamenco World

C/Huertas 62 ⊛www.flamenco-world.com. Mon–Sat 11am–2.30pm & 4.30–8pm. The place to come for flamenco CDs, DVDs and books. Helpful and highly knowledgeable staff. Check out the authoritative website too for all the latest news on new releases, up-coming concerts and emerging artists.

Fnac

C/Preciados 28. Mon–Sat 10am–9.30pm, Sun noon–9.30pm. French department store with excellent sections for books, videos, CDs and electrical equipment. Also sells concert tickets.

Mariano Madrueño

C/Postigo San Martín 3. Mon–Fri 9.30am–2pm & 5–8pm, Sat 9.30am–2pm. Great traditional wine seller's, established back in 1895, where there's an overpowering smell of grapes as you peruse its vintage-crammed shelves. Intriguing tipples include potent Licor de Hierbas from Galicia and home-made Pacharán (aniseed liqueur with sloe berries).

Seseña

C/Cruz 23. Mon–Sat 10am–1.30pm & 4.30–8pm. Open since 1901, this shop specializes in traditional Madrileño capes for royalty and celebrities. Clients have included Luis Buñuel, Gary Cooper and Hillary Clinton.

Cafés

Prado Cuatro

C/Prado 4. Daily 9am–2pm. This classic café has been given a modern makeover by its new owners, but it remains a relaxing place for a morning coffee, a lunch-time tapas or an evening cocktail.

La Mallorquina

Puerta del Sol 2. Daily 9am–9.15pm. Classic Madrid café, great for breakfast or sweet snacks. Try one of their *napolitanas* (cream slices) in the sunny upstairs salon that overlooks Puerta del Sol.

La Suiza

Plaza Santa Ana 2. Daily 7am–midnight. A traditional Madrid café serving delicious *leche merengada* (a sort of sweet whipped-milk ice cream) and a bewildering array of cakes. Its year-round terrace on the plaza is a perfect place to relax and watch the world go by.

Restaurants

El Cenador del Prado

C/Prado 4 ☎914 291 561. Mon–Sat 1.45–4pm & 9pm–midnight, Sun 1.45-4pm. Closed Aug. Relaxing, stylish decor and imaginative cuisine here, combining Spanish, Mediterranean and Far Eastern influences. There's an excellent-value *menú del día* served up for lunch and in the evening (Mon–Thurs only) as well as a children's menu at weekends (€12). If you want something a bit more special the €41 *menú de degustación* is a real treat and the desserts are spectacular.

Come Prima

C/Echegaray 27 ☎914 203 042. Mon 9pm–midnight, Tues–Sat 1.30–4pm & 9pm–midnight. Closed Aug. Superior Italian restaurant, with fresh ingredients, excellent antipasti and authentic main courses including a great seafood risotto. Very popular so make sure you book, and expect to pay around €35 a head.

Domine Cabra

C/Huertas 54 ☎914 294 365. Mon–Sat 2–4pm & 9–11.30pm, Sun 2–4pm. Closed Sat lunch & Sun in Aug &

first half of Sept. Interesting mix of traditional and modern, with *madrileño* standards given the *nueva cocina* (new cuisine) treatment. Sauces are tasty – a rarity in Spain – and presentation nice too. The *menú* at €16 is very good value and the service friendly.

La Finca de Susana

C/Arlabán 4 ⓦwww.lafinca-restaurant .com. Daily 1–3.45pm & 8.30–11.45pm. One of three great-value restaurants set up by a group of Catalan friends (another, *La Gloria de Montera* is just off Gran Vía, see p.115). A great *menú del día* for around €9, consists of simple dishes cooked with imagination. Stylish decor and quick, efficient service too, but arrive early to avoid queuing, as you can't book.

El Inti de Oro

C/Ventura de la Vega 12 ☎914 296 703. Daily 1.30–4pm & 8.30pm–midnight. Also at c/Amor de Dios 9 ☎914 291 958. The friendly staff at this good-value Peruvian restaurant are more than ready to provide suggestions for those new to the cuisine. The *pisco sour*, a cocktail of Peruvian liquor, lemon juice, egg white and sugar is a recommended starter, while the *cebiche de merluza* (raw fish marinated in lemon juice) is a wonderful dish. A full meal costs around €25.

Las Letras

C/Echegaray 26 ☎914 294 843. Tues–Sat 1.30–4pm & 9–11.30pm, Sun 1.30–4pm. Closed Aug and Sun in summer. Small informal bar/restaurant with designer touches to the decor and food. The constantly changing set menu usually contains a good selection of healthy and very tasty options at a competitive €10.50.

Lhardy

Carrera de San Jerónimo 8 ☎915 213 385, ⓦ www.lhardy.com. Restaurant: Mon–Sat 1–3.30pm & 9–11.30pm, Sun 1–3.30pm. Shop: Mon–Sat 9.30am–3pm & 5–9.30pm, Sun 9am–2.30pm. Once the haunt of royalty, this is one of Madrid's most beautiful and famous restaurants. It's greatly overpriced – expect to pay over €45 per head for a three-course meal – but on the ground floor, there's a wonderful bar/shop where you can snack on canapés, *fino* and *consommé*, without breaking the bank.

Mezklum Tech

C/Príncipe 16 ☎915 218 911, ⓦ www .mezklum.com. Mon–Sat 1–4pm & 9pm–midnight, Fri & Sat open till 1am. A self-consciously cool and chic arrival on the Santa Ana scene. Mezklum is decked out in minimalist style with white, pink and lilac tones and serves a fine array of Mediterranean dishes with good salads and pasta and stylish presentation. It has two good-value lunch-time menus at €10.90 and €14.90, while evening meals will cost around €25-30.

Paradis erReeFe

Palacio de Linares, Paseo de Recoletos 2 ☎915 754 540. 1–4pm and 9pm–midnight. Closed Sat lunch, Sun & Aug. This place has a wonderful setting in the Palacio de Linares, and specializes in Mediterranean rice dishes. Try the excellent *arroz negro* with seafood and expect to pay around €40 a head. The original branch is nearby at c/Marqués de Cubas 14 (☎914 297 303).

Le Petit Bistrot

Plaza Matute 5 ☎914 296 265 ⓦ www.lepetitbistrot.net. Tues–Sat 1.15–3.45pm & 9.15–11.45pm, Sun 11.30–2.30pm. A genuine French bistro in a quiet plaza just off Huertas. There's a very good €12.50 set lunch (€16.50 on Sat) and a hefty €18 brunch on Sundays. Classics such as French onion soup, steak in béarnaise sauce and profiteroles dripping in chocolate are all served up in a pleasant, relaxed atmosphere.

Prada A Tope

C/Príncipe 11 ☎914 295 921. Tues–Sun 12.30–5pm & 8pm–midnight. Quality produce from the El Bierzo region of León. The *morcilla* (black pudding), *empanada* (pasty) and *tortilla* are extremely tasty, while the smooth house wines provide the ideal accompaniment.

Suite Café Club

C/Virgen de los Peligros 4 ☎ 915 214 031, ⓦ www.suitecafeclub.com. Mon–Sat 1.30–4.30pm & 8.30pm–1am. Another one for the cool crowd, this restaurant/club serves an imaginative €11 set lunch and an even more creative €30 *menú de degustación* for dinner, often with good vegetarian options. In the evening, the front area becomes a cocktail bar and is a great place to start off a night on the tiles.

La Vaca Verónica

C/Moratín 38 ☎914 297 827. Mon–Fri 2–4pm & 9pm–midnight, Sat 9pm–midnight. A wide range of dishes is available at this amiable little restaurant, from Argentinian-style meat and fresh pasta in imaginative sauces, to quality fish and tasty vegetables. Try the *Filet Verónica* and the *carabinero con pasta* (pasta with red prawns). The *menú del día* is a reasonable €15.

Zerain

C/Quevedo 3. Mon–Sat 1.30–4pm & 8.30pm–midnight. Closed Aug.

Basque cider house and restaurant tucked away in a back street near Huertas serving excellent meat and fish dishes. The *chuletón* (T-bone steak) is the speciality, but it also does a very good *tortilla de bacalao* (cod tortilla) and grilled *rape* (monkfish).

Tapas bars

El Abuelo

C/Núñez de Arce 5. Wed–Sun 11.30am–3.30pm & 6.30–11.30pm. There's a *comedor* (dining room) at the back of this inexpensive bar, where you can order a selection of traditional *raciones* – the *croquetas* are especially good – and a jug of house wine.

Las Bravas

C/Alvarez Gato 3. Other branches at c/Espoz y Mina 13 and Pasaje Mathéu 5. Daily noon–4pm and 7pm–midnight. Standing-room only at these three bars, where, as the name suggests, *patatas bravas* are the thing to try. In fact, *Las Bravas* has patented its own version of the spicy sauce.

Casa del Abuelo

C/Victoria 12. Daily 11.30am–3.30pm & 6.30–11.30pm. A tiny, highly atmospheric bar serving just their own cloyingly sweet red wine and cooked prawns – try them *al ajillo* (in garlic) or *a la plancha* (fried). Use your free wine voucher to get a drink at the nearby sister bar, *El Abuelo* (see above).

Casa Alberto

C/Huertas 18 ☎914 299 356, ⓦwww .casaalberto.es. Tues–Sat noon–1am, Sun noon–4pm (in summer). Traditional *tasca* with a zinc and marble bar that has resisted the passage of time since it was founded back in 1827. Good *caracoles* (snails), *gambas* (prawns) and great *croquetas*, ideally accompanied by a glass of house vermouth.

Casa Labra

C/Tetuán 12 ☎915 310 081. Mon–Sat 11am–3.30pm & 5.30–11pm. Dating from 1869 – and where the Spanish Socialist Party was founded ten years later – this traditional and highly popular place retains much of its original interior. Order a drink at the

▼ CASA ALBERTO

bar and a *ración* of *bacalao* (cod fried in batter) or some of the best *croquetas* in town. There's also a restaurant at the back serving classic Madrileño food.

Casienhuertas

C/Lope de Vega 20. Tues–Fri 5pm–1am, Sat noon–5pm & 8.30pm–1am, Sun noon–5pm. A new arrival on the Huertas scene, this slickly decorated bar/restaurant has a short but select menu of sophisticated modern tapas. Dishes include delights such as courgette in tempura with raspberry and mango sauce. The cheeses are good too and all accompanied by a carefully selected wine list.

Museo del Jamón

Carrera de San Jerónimo 6. Mon–Sat 9am–midnight, Sun 10am–midnight. This is the largest branch of this Madrid chain, from whose ceilings are suspended hundreds of *jamones* (hams). The best – and they're not cheap – are the *jabugos* from the Sierra Morena, though a filling ham sandwich is only around €5.

La Oreja de Oro

C/Victoria 9. May–July & Sept Mon–Sat 1–4pm & 8pm–1am; Oct–April Tues–Sun 1–4pm & 8pm–1am. Closed Aug. Standing room only in this spit-and-sawdust bar. Try the excellent *pulpo a la Gallega* (sliced octopus served on a bed of potatoes seasoned with cayenne pepper) washed down with Ribeiro wine. Plenty of other seafood tapas on offer too.

La Trucha

C/Manuel Fernández y González 3 ℡914 295 833. Branch at nearby c/Nuñez de Arce 6 ℡915 320 890. Mon–Sat 12.30–4pm & 7.30pm–midnight. Closed Sun. Ever popular and usually crowded tapas

bar cum moderately priced restaurant, where delicious smoked fish and *pimientos de Padrón* are the specialities.

Viña P

Plaza de Santa Ana 3. Daily 1–4pm & 8pm–12.30am. Touristy but friendly bar decked out with bullfighting paraphernalia and serving a great range of tapas. Try the asparagus, stuffed mussels and the mouthwatering *almejas a la marinera* (clams in a garlic and white wine sauce).

Bars

Alhambra

C/Victoria 9. Daily noon–2am. Closed Mon mornings. A friendly tapas bar by day, *Alhambra* transforms itself into a fun disco bar by night with the crowds spilling over into the *El Buscón* bar next door.

Cervecería Alemana

Plaza de Santa Ana 6. Mon & Wed–Sun 10.30am–12.30am, Fri & Sat till 2am. Refurbished but still stylish old beer house, once frequented by Hemingway. Order a *caña* (draught beer) and go easy on the tapas, as the bill can mount up fast.

Cervecería Santa Ana

Plaza de Santa Ana 10. Daily 11am–1.30am, Fri & Sat till 2.30am. Cheaper than the *Alemana*, with tables outside, and offering quality beer, friendly service, and a good selection of tapas. Always packed at night.

Círculo de Bellas Artes

C/Alcalá 42. Daily 8am–2am, Fri & Sat till 3am. A stylish bar in this classy arts centre, complete with reclining nude sculpture, chandeliers and sofas, and a

▲ CÍRCULO DE BELLAS ARTES

pleasant lack of pretensions. Service can be slow though. From May to October there's a comfortable *terraza* outside.

The Glass Bar

Carrera San Jeronimo 34. Daily 11am–3am. Housed in the ultra-chic five-star *Hotel Urban*, this glamorous glass-fronted cocktail bar has become a compulsory stop for the well-heeled in-crowd. Designer tapas such as sushi, wild salmon and oysters are on offer to accompany drinks. In summer a terrace bar opens on the sixth floor.

Naturbier

Plaza de Santa Ana 9. Daily 8pm–2.30am. Try this place's own tasty beer with a variety of German sausages to accompany it. There's usually room to sit in the cellar if the top bar is too crowded, although service is often slow.

La Venencia

C/Echegaray 7. Daily 7.30pm–1.30am. Closed Aug. Rather dilapidated, wood-panelled bar that's great for sherry sampling. The whole range is here, served from wooden barrels, and accompanied by delicious olives and *mojama* (dry salted tuna). Atmospheric and authentic.

Viva Madrid

C/Manuel Fernández y González 7 ⓦ www.barvivamadrid.com. Daily noon–2am, Fri & Sat till 3am. A fabulous tiled bar – both outside and in – offering cocktails, beer and speciality coffees, plus basic tapas. Get here early if you want to see the tiles in their full glory, as it gets very crowded. Quite pricey, but certainly worth a stop.

Discobares and clubs

La Boca del Lobo

C/Echegaray 11 ⓦ www.labocadellobo .com. Wed–Sat 10.30pm–3.30am. Dark, cavern-like club on this buzzing little street close to Santa Ana playing everything from electronic and funk to rock and salsa. Live gigs (in the dungeon-like cellar) and resident DJs.

▲ LA VENENCIA

The Room/Mondo at Stella

C/Arlabán 7 ⓦwww
.web-mondo
.com. Thurs–Sat
1–6am. Entrance
€12–15 including
first drink. Now
unrecognizable
from its days
as a *Movida*
classic, *Stella* has
undergone a
complete make-
over to become a
cool modern club
with transparent
dance floor. It
remains a big
favourite with
the city's serious
party-goers,
especially for the
Room (Fri) and *Mondo* (Thurs &
Sat) sessions.

▲ LIVELY HUERTAS

Torero

C/Cruz 26. Tues–Sat 11pm–5.30am
(4.30am Wed). Very popular two-
floored club right in the heart
of the Santa Ana area. Normally
there is no entry fee, but the
bouncers are pretty strict and
you have to be reasonably well
dressed to get in. Music ranges
from salsa to disco.

Live music

Café Central

Plaza del Ángel 10 ☏913 694 143,
ⓦwww.cafecentralmadrid.com.
Mon–Sat 1pm–1.30am, Fri & Sat till
2.30am. €9–11 for gigs, otherwise
free. Small and relaxed jazz club
that gets the odd big name, plus
strong local talent. The Art Deco
café, which does a €10 lunch-
time menu, is worth a visit in its
own right.

Café Jazz Populart

C/Huertas 22 ☏914 298 407, ⓦwww
.populart.es. Daily 6pm–2.30am. Live
music supplement €6. Another
friendly and laid-back venue,
with twice-nightly sets (11pm &
12.30am) usually from jazz and
blues bands.

Cardamomo

C/Echegaray 15 ⓦwww.cardamomo
.net. Daily 9pm–4am. Noisy and fun
flamenco bar with a jam session
every Wednesday at 10.30pm
in an unpretentious atmosphere
that couldn't be more different
from the formal *tablaos*. No
entry charge and drinks are
standard prices.

The Paseo del Arte

Madrid's three world-class art galleries are all located within a kilometre of each other along what is commonly known as the Paseo del Arte.

The Prado is the most renowned of the three, housing an unequalled display of Spanish art, an outstanding Flemish collection and an impressive assemblage of Italian work. The Thyssen-Bornemisza, based on one of the world's greatest private art collections, provides an excursion through Western art from the fourteenth to the late twentieth centuries, excelling in all the areas in which the Prado is deficient. The final member of the trio, the Centro de Arte Reina Sofía, is an immense exhibition space, home to the Spanish collection of contemporary art, including the Miró and Picasso legacies and the jewel in the crown – Guernica.

If you're planning to visit all three galleries then pick up the Paseo del Arte ticket for €14.40 from any of the three. For souvenirs, each museum has excellent shops selling a range of gifts connected to both their own collections and to art in general.

Museo del Prado

Ⓦ www.museodelprado.es. Tues–Sun 9am–7pm, hols 9am–2pm. €6, free on Sun and for under-18s and over-65s. The Prado is Madrid's premier tourist attraction and one of the oldest and greatest collections of art in the world, largely amassed by the Spanish royal family – for the most part discerning and avid buyers – over the last two hundred years. Finding enough space for displaying the works has always been a problem, but after nearly fourteen years of arguments, delays and controversy, the new €152 million, Rafael Moneo–designed **extension**, which incorporates the reassembled eighteenth-century cloisters of the adjacent San Jerónimo church, has finally been completed. From the surface all you see is one new cube-like building and a patioed garden, but beneath lies a massive new wing which houses the **restaurant and café** areas, **shops**, an auditorium, temporary exhibition spaces, restoration and conservation workshops as well as a sculpture gallery. The new extension, which increases floor space by 50 percent, will free up room for more of the permanent collection to be displayed in the original Villanueva building and means no reorganization will be necessary for temporary shows.

The two original **entrances** to the museum: the Puerta de Goya, which has an upper and a lower entrance opposite the *Hotel Ritz* on c/Felipe IV, and the Puerta de Murillo on Plaza de Murillo, in front of the Botanical Gardens, have been complemented by two new entrances at either end

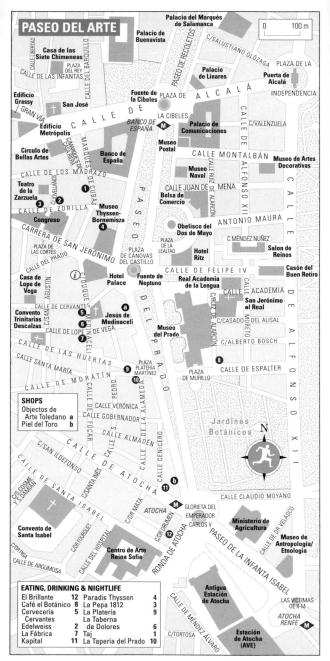

PASEO DEL ARTE

SHOPS
Objectos de
Arte Toledano a
Piel del Toro b

EATING, DRINKING & NIGHTLIFE
El Brillante 12   Paradis Thyssen   4
Café el Botánico 8   La Pepa 1812   3
Cervecería 5   La Platería   9
  Cervantes   La Taberna
Edelweiss 2   de Dolores   6
La Fábrica 7   Taj   1
Kapital 11   La Tapería del Prado 10

of the extension. It is worth checking to see which has the shorter queues. Rearrangements are inevitable as the collection is reorganized following the completion of the extension, but regularly updated **floor plans** are available at each entrance. If you want more background on the key paintings there are audio guides (€3.50) or informative general guides (€10.50 and €24.50) in the bookshop. The museum stages an increasing number of heavy-weight **temporary exhibitions**, a stunning show on Tintoretto being a recent highlight.

The comprehensive coverage of **Spanish paintings** begins on the ground floor with some striking twelfth-century Romanesque frescoes. Beyond and continuing upstairs is a stunning anthology that includes just about every significant Spanish painter from the adopted Cretan-born artist El Greco (Domenikos Theotocopulos), who worked in Toledo in the 1570s, to Francisco de Goya, the outstanding painter of eighteenth-century Bourbon Spain. Don't miss the breathtaking collection of work by Diego Velázquez, including

his masterpiece, *Las Meninas*, on the first floor (see box opposite).

Nor would any visit be complete without seeing Goya's deeply evocative works, *Dos de Mayo* and *Tres de Mayo*, and his disturbing series of murals known as the *Pinturas Negras* (*Black Paintings*) with their mix of witches, fights to the death and child-eating gods.

The **Italian paintings** include the most complete collection by painters from the Venice school in any single museum, among them Titian's magnificent equestrian portrait, *Emperor Carlos V at Mühlberg*. There are major works by Raphael and epic masterpieces from Tintoretto, Veronese, and Caravaggio too.

The early **Flemish works** are even more impressive and contain one of Hieronymus Bosch's greatest triptychs, the hallucinogenic *Garden of Earthly Delights*. Look out, too, for the works of Pieter Brueghel the Elder, whose *Triumph of Death* must be one of the most frightening canvases ever painted, Rogier van der Weyden's magnificent *Descent from the Cross*, and the extensive Rubens collection.

▲ ONE OF GOYA'S *BLACK PAINTINGS*

Las Meninas

One of the Prado's most-prized treasures, Velázquez's *Las Meninas* has been admired by public and artists alike since it was completed in 1656. Manet remarked of it, "After this I don't know why the rest of us paint"; the French poet Gautier asked, "But where is the picture?" because it seemed to him a continuation of the room; while the Italian painter, Luca Giordano, identified it as "the Theology of Painting".

Velázquez's skill as a portraitist had been recognized in 1623 when he was made court artist and established himself in Madrid. Painted more than thirty years later, his most famous work captures a moment in the artist's study, featuring Velázquez himself, the Infanta Margarita, various royal attendants, and Felipe IV and his wife, Mariana of Austria – standing in the viewer's position – reflected in the mirror on the wall. The artist's superlative brushwork and his mastery of colour, light and perspective mark the piece out as one of the all-time great works of art and secure Velázquez's reputation as Spain's most accomplished painter.

▲ STATUE OF VELAZQUEZ OUTSIDE THE PRADO

German and **French** painting is less well represented but still worth seeking out – especially the pieces by Dürer, Poussin and Lorrain – while downstairs in the basement is a glittering display of the **jewels** that belonged to the Grand Dauphin Louis, son of Louis XIV and father of Felipe V, Spain's first Bourbon king.

Museo Thyssen-Bornemisza

Ⓦ www.museothyssen.org. Tues–Sun 10am–7pm. €6 for permanent collection, €5 for temporary exhibitions, combined ticket €9. Free for under-12s.
This fabulous private collection, assembled by Baron Heinrich Thyssen-Bornemisza, his son Hans Heinrich and his wife Carmen (former beauty queen and ex-wife of Tarzan actor Lex Barker), was first displayed here in 1993 and contains pieces by almost every major Western artist since the fourteenth century.

The **new extension**, built on the site of an adjoining mansion and cleverly integrated into the original format of the museum, houses temporary exhibitions and Carmen's collection, which is particularly strong on nineteenth-century landscape, North American, Impressionist and Post-Impressionist work.

The museum **shop** stocks a range of informative books on the leading artists, while audio guides (€5) are available at the desk in the main hall.

To follow the collection chronologically, begin on the **second floor** with pre-Renaissance work from the fourteenth century. This is followed by a wonderful array of Renaissance portraits by, amongst others, Ghirlandaio, Raphael and Holbein, including the latter's commanding *Henry VIII*. Beyond are some equally impressive pieces by Titian, Tintoretto, El

▲ MUSEO THYSSEN-BORNEMISZA

Greco, Caravaggio and Canaletto, while a superb collection of landscapes and some soothing Impressionist works by Pissarro, Monet, Renoir, Degas and Sisley are housed in the new galleries.

The **first floor** continues with an evocative series of white marble sculptures by Rodin and an outstanding selection of work by Gauguin and the Post-Impressionists. There's excellent coverage, too, of the vivid Expressionist work of Kandinsky, Nolde and Kirchner.

Beyond, the displays include a comprehensive round of seventeenth-century Dutch painting of various genres and some splendid nineteenth-century American landscapes. There are strong contributions from Van Gogh – most notably one of his last and most gorgeous works, *Les Vessenots* – and more from the Expressionists, including the apocalyptic *Metropolis* by George Grosz.

The **ground floor** covers the period from the beginning of the twentieth century through to around 1970. Outstanding Cubist work from Picasso, Braque and Mondrian is to be found within the "experimental avant-garde" section. Look out, too, for some marvellous pieces by Miró, Pollock and Chagall. Surrealism is, not surprisingly, represented by Dalí, while the final galleries include some eye-catching work by Bacon, Lichtenstein and Freud.

Centro de Arte Reina Sofía

ⓦwww.museoreinasofia.es. Mon & Wed–Sat 10am–9pm, Sun 10am–2.30pm. €6, free Sat after 2.30pm & all day Sun and for under-18s and over-65s. The other essential stop on the Madrid art circuit is the Centro de Arte Reina Sofía, an immense exhibition space providing a permanent home for the Spanish collection of modern and contemporary art.

The museum, a vast former hospital, has undergone a €79 million extension programme that has added a state-of-the-art metal and glass triangular-shaped wing designed by French architect Jean Nouvel behind the main block, allowing more space for temporary exhibitions.

An informative **guide** is available from the shop (€17) and there are audio guides (€4) at the entrance.

The permanent collection begins on the **second floor** with a section examining the origins of modern Spanish art, largely through the two artistic nuclei that developed in Catalunya and the Basque Country at the end of the nineteenth century.

Midway round the collection is the Reina Sofía's main draw – Picasso's *Guernica* (see box), an emblematic piece that has always evoked strong reactions.

Strong sections on Cubism and the Paris School follow, in the first of which Picasso is again well represented. Dalí and Miró make heavyweight contributions too in the Surrealism section, while an impressive collection of Spanish sculpture is to be found in the final rooms.

The collection continues on the **fourth floor**, although here it's no match for the attractions of the previous exhibits. This section covers Spain's postwar years up to the present day and includes Spanish and international examples of abstract and avant-garde movements

▲ REINA SOFIA

such as Pop Art, Constructivism and Minimalism, one of the highlights being Francis Bacon's *Figura Tumbada* (*Reclining Figure*).

There are also some striking pieces by the Basque abstract sculptor, Chillida, and Catalan Surrealist painter Antoni Tàpies.

The extension, or **Area Nouvel**, is built around an open courtyard topped by a striking delta-shaped, metallic, crimson-coloured roof. It is home to the temporary exhibition spaces, an auditorium, a library and bookshop. Also housed in the new wing is *Arola Madrid*, a café/restaurant run under the auspices of leading Catalan chef Sergi Arola. Coffee and cakes are affordable despite the ridiculous ticket-ordering system, but lunch or supper will set you back at least €50.

Guernica

Superbly displayed and no longer protected by bullet-proof glass and steel girders, Picasso's *Guernica* is a monumental icon of twentieth-century Spanish art and politics which, despite its familiarity, still has the ability to shock. Picasso painted it in response to the bombing of the Basque town of Gernika in April 1937 by the German Luftwaffe, acting in concert with Franco, during the Spanish Civil War. In the preliminary studies, displayed around the room, you can see how he developed its symbols – the dying horse, the woman mourning, the bull and so on – and then return to the painting to marvel at how he made it all work. Picasso determined that the work be "loaned" to the Museum of Modern Art in New York while Franco remained in power, meaning that the artist never lived to see it displayed in his home country – it only returned to Spain in 1981, eight years after Picasso's death and six after the demise of Franco.

Shops

Objectos de Arte Toledano
Paseo del Prado 10. Mon–Sat 9.30am–
8pm. All-purpose souvenir shop
stocking "typical Spanish"-style
goods including fans, Lladró
porcelain, T-shirts and tacky
flamenco accessories.

Piel del Toro
Paseo del Prado 42. Mon–Fri
10am–8.30pm, Sat & Sun 11am–8pm.
A colourful range of T-shirts,
sweatshirts and baseball caps, all
emblazoned with the emblem of
a bull. Despite the clichéd image
they make good, lightweight
presents.

Cafés

Café el Botánico
C/Ruiz de Alarcón 27. Daily 9am–
midnight. An ideal place for a
morning coffee or an afternoon
drink after a Prado visit, this
place serves good beer and
a small selection of delicious
canapés and tapas.

Restaurants

Edelweiss
C/Jovellanos 7 ☎915 323 383.
1–4pm & 8pm–midnight, closed
Sun eve. Quality German
restaurant with good service,
an authentic array of central
European specialities and
large portions. Expect to pay
around €35 a head, although
a more economical option is
the €20 lunch-time menu
which includes the obligatory
selection of *bratwürst*.

Paradis Thyssen
Paseo del Prado 8 ☎914 292 732
Tues–Sun 1–4.30pm. Lunch-time-
only restaurant, run by the
Paradis group, that is situated
in the courtyard of the Thyssen
museum and a good place for
food if you plan to make a day
of it at the galleries. A very
decent €11 *menú del día* but
not really worth the expense
of eating *à la carte*. There is a
pleasant summer-time terrace.

La Pepa 1812
C/Zorilla 7 ☎914 296 258. Mon–Tues
12.30–4pm, Wed–Sat 12.30–4pm &
8.30pm–midnight. Relatively new
arrival in this quiet street tucked
behind the Congreso. Does a
very good €11.50 set menu
with home-made specials and
offers interesting options such as
salmon burgers and goat's cheese
salad. Eating à la carte will cost
a reasonable €25.

Taj
C/Marqués de Cubas 6 ☎915 315
059. Daily 1–4pm & 8.30pm–midnight.
Friendly service in this
traditional curry house. Does
some good starters and a tasty
chicken tikka masala. Prices are
pretty reasonable too at around
€25–30 a head.

La Tapería del Prado
Plaza Platerías de Martínez 1 ☎914
294 094. Daily 7.30am–12.30am.
Modern, slightly pricey bar
serving up an inventive range
of tapas and *raciones*, plus a
decent set lunch at around €10.
Portions are on the small side
though.

Tapas bars

El Brillante
Glorieta del Emperador Carlos V 8.
Daily 6.30am–12.30am. Popular,
down-to-earth bar, with long
opening hours and a wide
range of tapas and *bocadillos*

(filled baguette) – *calamares* is the house special – making it a great place for a quick snack in between museum visits.

Cervecería Cervantes

Plaza de Jesús 7. Mon–Sat 12.30–5pm & 7.30–11.45pm, Sun noon–4pm. Great beer and excellent fresh seafood tapas in this busy kitchen-like bar. The *gambas* (prawns) go down a treat with a cool glass of the beer, while the *tosta de gambas* (a sort of prawn toast) is a must.

La Fábrica

Plaza de Jesús 2. Mon–Thurs & Sun 11am–1am, Fri & Sat 11am–2am. Bustling, friendly bar serving a delicious range of canapés, chilled beer and good vermouth. There's seating at the back for tapas if you want to linger for longer.

La Platería

C/Moratín 49. Mon–Fri 7.30am–1am, Sat & Sun 9.30am–1am. This bar has an enormously popular summer *terraza* and a good selection of reasonably priced tapas available at any time of the day. Service can be a little brusque though.

La Taberna de Dolores

Plaza de Jesús 4. Daily 11am–midnight. The canapés are splendid at this popular standing-room-only tiled bar, decorated with beer bottles from around the world. The

▲ TILED FRONTAGE OF LA TABERNA DE DOLORES

beer on offer is really good and the food specialities include Roquefort and anchovy, and smoked-salmon canapés.

Club

Kapital

C/Atocha 125 ⓦ www.grupo-kapital .com. Open Thurs–Sun midnight–6am. From €12. Seven-floor macroclub catering for practically every taste with three dance floors, lasers, go-go dancers, a cinema and a top-floor *terraza*. Varied musical menu of disco, merengue, salsa, *sevillanas* and even some karaoke, plus its own "after hours" session from 8pm on Sundays.

The Retiro and around

The area around the Paseo del Prado is the site of two of the city's most beautiful green spaces: the peaceful Jardines Botánicos and the Parque del Retiro, a delightful mix of formal gardens and wider open spaces. The district is also home to a host of lesser-known sights, from the impressively renovated Estación de Atocha to a number of small museums, including the fascinating Real Fábrica de Tapices (Royal Tapestry Workshop). It isn't an area renowned for its bars, restaurants and nightlife, but there are still enough decent places for a drink or lunch-time pitstop.

Parque del Retiro

The origins of the wonderful Parque del Retiro (Retiro Park) go back to the early seventeenth century when Felipe IV produced a plan for a new palace and French-style gardens, the Buen Retiro. Of the buildings, only the ballroom (Casón del Buen Retiro) and the Hall of Realms (the former Museo del Ejército) remain.

The park itself has been public property for over a hundred years. Its 330-acre expanse offers the chance to jog, rollerblade, cycle, picnic, row on the lake (you can rent boats by the Monumento a Alfonso XII), have your fortune told, and – above all – promenade. The busiest day is Sunday, when half of Madrid turns out for the *paseo* and there are plenty of stalls and cafés for snack breaks.

Promenading aside, there's almost always something going on in the park, including concerts in the Quiosco de Música, performances by groups

▲ RETIRO PARK BOATING LAKE

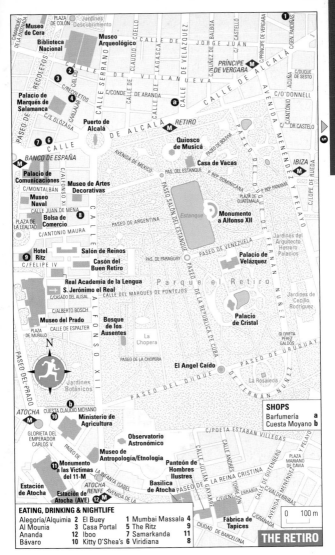

SHOPS
Barfumería **a**
Cuesta Moyano **b**

THE RETIRO

0   100 m

EATING, DRINKING & NIGHTLIFE

Alegoría/Alquimia	2	El Buey	1	Mumbai Massala	4
Al Mounia	3	Casa Portal	5	The Ritz	9
Ananda	12	Iboo	7	Samarkanda	11
Bávaro	10	Kitty O'Shea's	6	Viridiana	8

of South American musicians by the lake and, on summer weekends, puppet shows by the Puerta de Alcalá entrance.

Travelling **art exhibitions** are frequently housed in the graceful Palacio de Velázquez

(May–Sept Mon & Wed–Sat 11am–8pm, Sun 11am–6pm; Oct–April Mon & Wed–Sat 10am–6pm, Sun 10am–4pm; free), the splendid Palacio de Cristal (same hours; ☎915 746 614 for information;

free) and Casa de Vacas (daily 10.30am–2.30pm & 4–8pm; closed Aug; free). Look out, too, for the **Ángel Caído** (Fallen Angel), supposedly the world's only public statue to Lucifer, in the south of the park, and the magnificently ostentatious statue to Alfonso XII by the lake. There is also the **Bosque de los Ausentes**, 191 olive trees and cypresses planted by the Paseo de la Chopera in memory of the victims who died in the train bombings at the nearby Atocha station on March 11, 2004.

Puerta de Alcalá

The Puerta de Alcalá is one of Madrid's most emblematic landmarks. Built in Neoclassical style in 1769 by Francesco Sabatini to commemorate Carlos III's first twenty years on the throne, it was the biggest city gate in Europe at the time. Once on the site of the city's easternmost boundary, it's now

▼ BOTANICAL GARDENS

marooned on a small island on the traffic-filled Plaza de la Independencia.

Jardines Botánicos

Plaza de Murillo 2 ⓦ www.rjb.csic .es. Daily 10am–dusk. €2. The delightful and shaded Jardines Botánicos (Botanical Gardens) were opened in 1781 by Carlos III. The king's aim was to collect and grow species from all over his Spanish Empire, develop a research centre, and supply medicinal herbs and plants to Madrid's hospitals. However, the gardens were abandoned after the Peninsular War and, although they were renovated later in the nineteenth century and a zoo installed, they soon fell into disrepair once again. They were eventually restored in the 1980s, using the original eighteenth-century plans and are now home to some 30,000 species from around the globe. The collection of flora is fascinating for any amateur botanist and don't miss the hothouse with its tropical plants and amazing cacti or the bonsai collection of former prime minister Felipe González.

Museo de Artes Decorativas

C/Montalbán 12 ⓦ mnartesdecorativas .mcu.es. Tues–Sat 9.30am–3pm, Sun 10am–3pm. €2.40, free on Sun. The national collection of decorative arts is housed in a suitably aristocratic nineteenth-century mansion. The highlight is its collection of *azulejos* (tiles) and other ceramics with a magnificent eighteenth-century tiled Valencian kitchen on the top floor. The rest of the exhibits include an interesting but unspectacular collection of furniture, a series of reconstructed rooms and *objets d'art* from all over Spain.

▲ MUSEO DE ARTES DECORATIVAS

in the early sixteenth century by the Catholic monarchs, Fernando and Isabel. An important destination for religious processions, it also became the venue for the swearing-in of the heirs to the throne and setting for many royal marriages and coronations (including the current king, Juan Carlos, in 1975). Despite significant remodelling and two Gothic towers added in the mid-nineteenth century, the old form of the church is still clearly visible; but the seventeenth–century cloisters have fallen victim to the controversial Prado extension plan (see p.90).

Museo Naval

Paseo del Prado 5 ⓦ www .museonavalmadrid.com. Tues–Sun 10am–2pm; closed Aug and public hols. Free (bring ID). As you might expect, the Naval Museum is strong on models, charts and navigational aids relating to Spanish voyages of discovery. Exhibits include the first map to show the New World, drawn in 1500; cannons from the Spanish Armada; part of Cortés' standard used during the conquest of Mexico; and some giant, late seventeenth-century globes. The room dedicated to the *Nao San Diego*, which was sunk during a conflict with the Dutch off the Philippines in 1600, contains fascinating items recovered during the salvage operation in the early 1990s.

San Jerónimo el Real

C/Ruiz de Alarcón 19. Mon–Fri 8am–1.30pm & 6–8pm, Sat & Sun 9am–1.30pm & 6.30–8pm, Oct–July opens one hour earlier in the afternoon. Madrid's high-society church was built on the site of a monastery founded

Real Academia Española de la Lengua

C/Ruiz de Alarcón 17. Fronted by a suitably imposing Neoclassical portico, the Royal Language Academy was established in 1714 by Felipe V to "cultivate and establish the purity and elegance of the Castilian language". Its job nowadays is to make sure that Spanish is not corrupted by foreign or otherwise unsuitable words and the academy's results are entrusted to their official dictionary – a work that bears virtually no relation to the Spanish spoken on the streets.

Plaza de la Lealtad

This aristocratic semicircular plaza contains the **Monumento a los Caídos por España** (Monument to Spain's Fallen). Originally a memorial to the Madrileños who died in the 1808 anti-French rebellion (the urn at the base contains the ashes of those killed), it was later changed to commemorate all those who have died fighting for Spain, and an eternal flame

▲ MONUMENTO A LOS CAÍDOS POR ESPAÑA

now burns here. On one side of the plaza stands the opulent *Ritz Hotel* (see pp.105 & 169), work of Charles Mewès, architect of the *Ritz* hotels in Paris and London. Opposite is the elegant colonnaded Bolsa de Comercio (Spain's stock exchange).

Estación de Atocha

The grand Estación de Atocha is now sadly infamous as the scene of the horrific train bombings that killed 191 people and injured close to 2000 in March 2004. A translucent glass **memorial** to the victims stands just outside one of the entrances on Paseo de la Infanta Isabel. The tower channels light into an underground chamber (access via the station) lined with an inner membrane on which are written messages of condolence.

The **old station** alongside was revamped in 1992 and is a glorious 1880s glasshouse, resembling a tropical garden. It's a wonderful sight from the walkways above, as a constant spray of water rains down on the jungle of vegetation. On the platforms beyond sit the gleaming high-speed AVE trains.

Ministerio de Agricultura

Glorieta del Emperador Carlos V.
Overblown and hard to miss, the Ministry of Agriculture was designed in 1893 to epic proportions. Its exterior features decorative tile work and monumental caryatids representing Industry and

▲ ATOCHA STATION INTERIOR GARDEN

Agriculture, while the whole thing is crowned with a striking figure of Glory, flanked by winged horses.

Museo Nacional de Antropología/ Etnología

C/Alfonso XII 68 ⓦ mnantropologia .mcu.es. Tues–Sat 10am–8pm, Sun 10am–3pm. €2.40, free Sat after 2.30pm & Sun.

▲ REAL FÁBRICA DE TAPICES

The National Anthropology and Ethnography Museum was founded by the eccentric Dr Pedro González Velasco to house his private collection. The generally unimaginative displays give an overview of different cultures, in particular those linked to Spanish history. The most interesting exhibits are in a side room on the ground floor – a macabre collection of deformed skulls, a Guanche mummy (the original inhabitants of the Canary Islands), shrivelled embryos and the skeleton of a circus giant (2.35m tall) from whom Velasco had agreed to buy the skeleton after his death – payment in advance of course.

Real Fábrica de Tapices

C/Fuentarrabía 2 ⓦ www .realfabricadetapices.com. Mon–Fri 10am–2pm; closed Aug. €3. Tours every half hour (guides usually speak English). The Royal Tapestry Workshop makes for a fascinating visit. Founded in 1721 and moved to its present site in the nineteenth century, the factory uses processes and machines unchanged for hundreds of years, including original eighteenth-century vertical looms. The workers, now numbering around 75 compared to four hundred half a century ago, can be seen coolly looping handfuls of bobbins around myriad strings, sewing up worn-out masterpieces with exact matching silk, and weaving together different shades for a new tapestry. With progress being painfully slow – one worker produces a square metre of tapestry every three and a half months – the astronomical prices soon seem easily understandable. One of the giant sixteenth-century Flemish tapestries on display took more than two generations to complete.

Panteón de Hombres Ilustres

C/Julián Gayarre 3 ⓦ www .patrimonionacional.es. April–Sept Mon–Sat 9am–7pm, Sun 9am–4pm; Oct–March Mon–Sat 9.30am–6pm, Sun 9am–3pm. Free. Built adjacent to the Real Basílica de Atocha, this late eighteenth-century Byzantine-style building was meant to serve as a mausoleum for the most important figures in Madrid's history. The full extent of the plans was never realized and many of the bodies have since been removed. There are, however, some impressively elaborate marble tombs commemorating nineteenth-century politicians, many of whom were assassinated during this turbulent period in the city's history.

Shops

Barfumería

C/Conde de Aranda 44 (basement). ⓦwww.barfumeria.com. A perfume shop with a difference, selling the fragrances on the basis of the aromas they produce (citrus, spice and floral) rather than the names of companies that make them. Also sells perfumes for the house.

Cuesta Moyano

Cuesta de Claudio Moyano. A row of little wooden kiosks located on the recently spruced up hill close to the Retiro selling just about every book you could think of, from second-hand copies of Captain Marvel to Cervantes or Jackie Collins. Apart from the books, there's always something of interest, such as old prints of Madrid and relics from the Franco era.

▼ BOOK STALLS ON CUESTA MOYANO

Restaurants

Al Mounia

C/Recoletos 5 ☎914 350 828. Tues–Sat 1.30–3.30pm & 9pm–midnight. Closed Aug. Moroccan cooking at its best in the most established Arabic restaurant in town, offering an atmospheric and romantic setting with impeccable service. The couscous and desserts are a must, but prices are high with main courses costing around €20.

El Buey

C/General Pardiñas 10 ☎914 314 492. Mon–Sat 1–4pm & 9pm–midnight, Sun 1–4pm. Excellent Argentine-style meat dishes in this cramped little restaurant near the Retiro. Prices – €30–35 per person – are pretty reasonable considering the high quality.

Casa Portal

C/Dr Castelo 26 ☎915 742 026 ⓦwww.casa-portal.com. Tues–Sat 1.30–4pm & 8.30–11.30pm. Closed hols & Aug. Superlative Asturian cooking – go for the *fabada* (beans, *chorizo* and black pudding stew) or *besugo* (bream), washed down with some cider. The shellfish is excellent too. Around €35-40 per person.

Iboo

C/Alcalá 55 ☎917 811 555. Mon–Fri 8am–midnight, Sat 11am–midnight, Sun 11am–4pm. A fast-food restaurant with a difference. Run by the prestigious Spanish chef Mario Sandoval, the *Iboo* chain specializes in quality Mediterranean cuisine at affordable prices. The *menú del día* is very good value at €10.50. There is another branch at c/Genova 4, near Alonso Martínez.

Mumbai Massala

C/Recoletos 14 ☎914 357 194, ⓦwww
.mumbaimassala.com. Daily 1.30–4pm
& 9–11.30pm. The decor is
palatial in this upmarket Indian
restaurant, serving a wide range
of very good, but expensive,
curries – all the usual favourites
are available. Evening prices are
in the region of €37 a head, but
a better alternative is the lunch-
time menu for just €12.

Samarkanda

Estación de Atocha ☎915 309 746.
Daily 1.30–4pm & 9pm–midnight.
Light years away from the
typical fare at your average
railway station, this colonial-style
restaurant, perched alongside the
tropical garden, serves excellent
and imaginative dishes – such as
ostrich steak in sweet and sour
sauce – in a great setting. It can,
however, get unbearably hot
in summer. Main courses cost
€14–17 or there's also a small
café for a drink and a snack.

Viridiana

C/Juan de Mena 14 ☎915 234 478 or
915 311 039 ⓦwww
.restauranteviridiana.com. Mon–Sat
1.30–4pm & 8.30pm–midnight.
Closed Easter & Aug. A bizarre
temple of Madrid *nueva cocina*
(new cuisine), decorated with
photos from Luis Buñuel's film
of the same name and offering
mouthwatering creations from
a constantly changing menu,
plus a superb selection of wines.
The bill is likely to come to
around €75 a head but it's an
unforgettable experience.

Bars

Bávaro

Cuesta Claudio Moyano. Daily noon–
3am. Perched on a little island
of grass and with views towards

Atocha, this summer *terraza*
makes a great stop at any time
of the day or night.

Kitty O'Shea's

C/Alcalá 59. Mon–Thurs & Sun
11am–2am, Fri & Sat 11am–3am.
Spacious Irish bar offering the
usual mixture of Irish beers and
TV sports, plus plenty of very
reasonable pub-style food.

The Ritz

Plaza de la Lealtad 5. Breakfast 7.30–
11am, tea 4.30–7.30pm, drinks and
tapas 7.30pm–1am. For a glimpse
of how the other half live, try
afternoon English-style tea or
early-evening cocktails in the
luxurious surroundings of the
Ritz, if you can afford the prices
that is.

Discobares and clubs

Alegoría/Alquimia

C/Villanueva 2 (entrance on c/Cid)
☎915 772 785, ⓦwww.alegoria
-madrid.com. Daily 9pm–5am.

▼ ALEGORÍA

Entrance €9. Modelled on an English gentleman's club, this restaurant, bar and disco rolled into one comes complete with a wood-panelled library and models of old sailing ships. Dinner costs around €30-35.

Ananda

Avda Ciudad de Barcelona. ⓦwww .ananda.es. Terraza: May–Sept, daily midnight till dawn. Indoor club: Sept–May, Thurs–Sat 11pm–dawn. Ultra-cool club located at the back of Atocha station that has a glamorous clientele and a trendy summer *terraza* with oriental furnishings. Get here around midnight to grab one of the comfy white leather sofas and, if you don't fancy people-watching, there are often concerts, talent contests and exhibitions to keep you entertained.

Gran Vía, Chueca and Malasaña

The Gran Vía, one of Madrid's main thoroughfares, effectively divides the old city to the south from the newer parts in the north. Permanently heaving with traffic, shoppers and sightseers, it's the commercial heart of the city, and quite a monument in its own right, with its turn-of-the-twentieth-century, palace-like banks and offices, and the huge hand-painted posters of its cinemas. North of here, and bursting with bars, restaurants and nightlife, are two of the city's most characterful barrios: Chueca, focal point of Madrid's gay scene, and neighbouring Malasaña, former centre of the Movida Madrileña, the happening scene of the late 1970s and early 1980s, and still a somewhat alternative area, focusing on lively Plaza Dos de Mayo. As well as the bustling atmosphere, a couple of museums and a number of beautiful churches in the area provide even more reasons for a visit.

Gran Vía

The Gran Vía (Great Way) was built in three stages over nearly half a century and became a symbol of Spain's arrival in the twentieth century. Financed on the back of an economic boom, experienced as a result of the country's neutrality in World War I, the Gran Vía is a showcase for a whole gamut of architectural styles, from Modernist and Art Deco to Neo-Rococo and Rationalist.

The finest section is the earliest, constructed between 1910 and 1924 and stretching from c/Alcalá to the Telefónica skyscraper. Particularly noteworthy are the **Edificio Metrópolis** (1905–11), complete with cylindrical facade, white stone sculptures, zinc-tiled roof and gold garlands, and the nearby **Grassy** building (1916–17), which is equally extravagant.

Further along, the vast 81-metre-high slab of the **Telefónica** building, with its plain sand-coloured facade, was

▼ GRAN VÍA

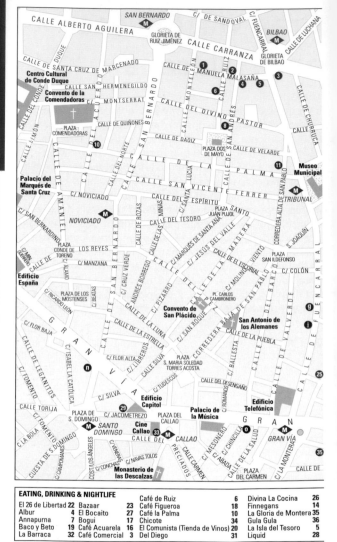

EATING, DRINKING & NIGHTLIFE						
El 26 de Libertad	22	Bazaar	23	Café de Ruiz	6	Divina La Cocina	26
Albur	4	El Bocaito	27	Café Figueroa	18	Finnegans	14
Annapurna	7	Bogui	17	Café la Palma	10	La Gloria de Montera	35
Baco y Beto	19	Café Acuarela	16	Chicote	34	Gula Gula	36
La Barraca	32	Café Comercial	3	El Comunista (Tienda de Vinos)	20	La Isla del Tesoro	5
				Del Diego	31	Liquid	28

Spain's first skyscraper. During
the Civil War, the building was
used as a reference point by
Franco's forces to bomb the
Gran Vía.

The stretch down to Plaza de
Callao is dominated by shops,
cafés and cinemas with their
massive hand-painted posters,
while the plaza itself is now the
gateway to the shoppers' paradise
of c/Preciados. On the corner
is the classic Art Deco **Capitol**
building (1930–33) – also

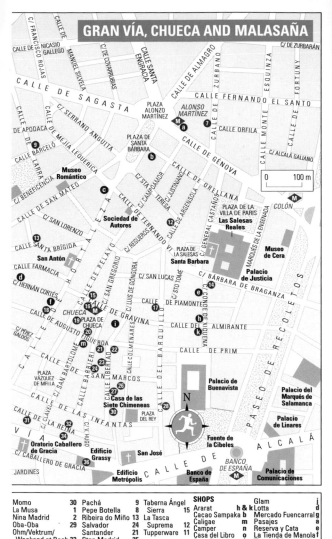

GRAN VÍA, CHUECA AND MALASAÑA

				SHOPS		Glam	j
Momo	30	Pachá	9	Taberna Ángel	Ararat h & k	Lotta	d
La Musa	1	Pepe Botella	8	Sierra 15	Cacao Sampaka b	Mercado Fuencarral	g
Nina Madrid	2	Ribeira do Miño	13	La Tasca	Caligae m	Pasajes	a
Oba-Oba	29	Salvador	24	Suprema 12	Camper n	Reserva y Cata	e
Ohm/Vektrum		Santander	21	Tupperware 11	Casa del Libro o	La Tienda de Manola	f
Weekend at Bash	33	Stop Madrid	25		Casa Postal i	Tienda Olivarero	c

known as the Edificio Carrion – its curved facade embellished with lurid neon signs.

Cast your eyes skywards on the final stretch downhill towards Plaza de España to catch site of an assortment of statues and decorations that top many of the buildings on this more modern section.

Plaza de Chueca

The smaller streets immediately north of Gran Vía are home

▲ PLAZA DE CHUECA

to all manner of vice-related activities and are notorious for petty crime. However, in Plaza de Chueca and the barrio around it there's a strong neighbourhood feel, with kids and grannies on the streets during the day, and a lively gay scene at night.

The area has been rejuvenated in recent years and from Plaza de Chueca east to Paseo de Recoletos you'll find some of the city's most enticing streets. Offbeat restaurants, small private art galleries and unusual corner shops are here in abundance. calle/Almirante has some of the city's most fashionable clothes shops and c/Augusto Figueroa is the place to go if you're looking for shoes.

La Casa de las Siete Chimeneas

Plaza del Rey 1. The sixteenth-century House of Seven Chimneys is allegedly haunted by an illegitimate daughter of Felipe II who disappeared in mysterious circumstances. The building – which now houses offices belonging to the Ministry of Culture – has been heavily restored, but is still recognizable as the work of El Escorial architects, Juan Bautista de Toledo and Juan de Herrera, with its red-brick and slate turret. Charles I of England stayed here when he came to Madrid to press his unsuccessful suit for marriage to the Infanta María.

Las Salesas Reales

Plaza de Las Salesas. 9am–1.30pm & 6–9pm. The convent complex of Las Salesas Reales was founded in 1747 by Barbara of Bragança, Portuguese wife of Fernando VI.

Santa Barbara church, with its imposing Baroque facade decorated with marble statues, is set behind a fine forecourt containing a rose garden, palm trees and magnolias. Inside, there's a grotto-like chapel, delightful frescoes and stained-glass windows, an extravagant pulpit and striking green marble altar decoration. The elaborate tomb of Fernando VI lies in the main church, as does that of the military hero General O'Donnell, while Barbara herself has been relegated to a side chapel.

The convent behind the church now houses the Palacio

de Justicia, the city's Law Courts, facing the elegant Plaza de la Villa de París.

Sociedad de Autores

C/Fernando VI 4. Home to the Society of Authors, this is the most significant Modernista building in Madrid. Designed in 1902 by the Catalan architect José Grasés Riera, its facade features a dripping decoration of flowers, faces and balconies giving the appearance of a melting candle.

Plaza Dos de Mayo

Plaza Dos de Mayo is the centre of the lively Malasaña bar scene with customers spilling on to the streets that converge on the square. The plaza commemorates the rebellion against occupying French troops in 1808, while the neighborhood gets its name from a young seamstress, Manuela Malasaña, who became one of the rebellion's heroines. Legend has it that she was executed for carrying a weapon (her scissors) after she was searched by the occupiers on her way home from work.

Museo Romántico

C/San Mateo 13 ⓦ museoromantico .mcu.es. Closed for refurbishment until 2008, though usually open Tues–Sat 9am–3pm, Sun & hols 10am–2pm; closed Aug. €2.40, free on Sun. The Museo Romántico aims to show the lifestyles and ideas of the late-Romantic era through the re-creation of a typical period residence (the building itself dates back to the late eighteenth century). It's a pretty successful attempt, with its musty atmosphere, creaking floorboards, cracking walls crowded with canvases, and rooms overflowing with kitsch memorabilia and furniture.

Museo Municipal

C/Fuencarral 78 ⓦ www.munimadrid .es/museomunicipal. Partly closed for refurbishment (an interesting selection of key exhibits is on show in the chapel), though usually open Tues–Fri 9.30am–8pm, Sat & Sun 10am–2pm; Aug: Tues–Fri 9.30am–2pm, Sat & Sun 10am–2pm. Free. The Museo Municipal is housed in the former city almshouse, remodelled in the early eighteenth century by Pedro de Ribera, who gave it a fantastically decorated Baroque doorway placed on an otherwise plain red-brick facade.

Inside is a chronological collection of paintings, photos, models, sculptures and porcelain, all relating to the history and urban development of Madrid since 1561 (the date it was designated imperial capital by Felipe II) through to the twentieth century. The centre-piece is a fascinating 3-D model of the city made in 1830 by military engineer León Gil de Palacio.

The eighteenth-century **chapel** on the ground floor survives from the time de Ribera remodelled the building

▲ MUSEO MUNICIPAL

▲ FRESCOES INSIDE SAN ANTONIO DE LOS ALEMANES

and contains a dramatic canvas, *San Fernando ante la Virgen*, above the altar.

San Antonio de los Alemanes

Corredera de San Pablo 16. Daily 9am–1pm & 6–8pm. Free. One of the city's hidden treasures, this little church was designed in 1624 by the Jesuit architect, Pedro Sánchez, and Juan Gómez de Mora. The elliptical interior is lined with dizzying floor-to-ceiling pastel-coloured frescoes by Neapolitan artist Luca Giordano which depict scenes from the life of St Anthony.

Shops

Ararat

C/Almirante 10 & 11. Mon–Sat 11am–2pm & 5–8.30pm. Two shops with Spanish and foreign designers for men, women and children at reasonably modest prices. The women's shop at no. 10 specializes in more formal wear, while no. 11 goes for a younger, more modern look.

Cacao Sampaka

C/Orellana 4 ⓦ www.cacaosampaka .com. Mon–Sat 10am–9pm, Sun 11am–9pm. Closed Aug 8–21. Every conceivable colour, shape and flavour of chocolate is available in this chocoholics' paradise. There are even books about the stuff. The only surprise is that the restaurant has some non-chocolate snacks on the menu.

Caligae

C/Augusto Figueroa 27. Mon–Fri 10am–2pm & 5–8pm, Sat 10.30am–2pm & 5–8pm. One of a string of shoe shops located on this busy Chueca street selling discounted designer footwear. If you're on the lookout for some sandals, fashion trainers, party shoes or boots, then this is the place to come.

Camper

C/Gran Vía 54 ⓦ www.camper.es Mon–Sat 10am–2pm & 5–8.30pm. Spain's best shoe-shop chain, selling practical and comfortable designs at modest prices, with the odd quirky fabric and unusual heel thrown in. There are lots of other branches around the city.

Casa del Libro

Gran Vía 29 and c/Maestro Victoria 3. ⓦ www.casadellibro.com. Mon–Sat 9.30am–9.30pm. The Casa del Libro's Gran Vía branch is the city's biggest bookshop, with four floors covering just about everything, including a wide range of fiction in English and translations of classic Spanish works. The branch at Maestro Victoria has a good section of maps, guides and books about Madrid.

Casa Postal

C/Libertad 37. Mon–Fri 10am–2pm & 5–8.30pm, Sat 10.30am–2pm. Marvellous old-fashioned shop for lovers of nostalgia, packed with postcards, posters and other original mementos of the city.

Glam

C/Fuencarral 35 ⓦwww.glam
.es. Mon–Fri 11am–9pm, Sat
11am–9.30pm, Sun 4.30–9pm.
Club/street-style clothes that
wouldn't look out of place in
an Almodóvar film. Good-value
shirts and tops too. There's a
shoe shop with wacky trainers
and trendy footwear next door.

Lotta

C/Hernán Cortés 9. Mon–Sat 11am–
2pm & 5–9pm. Named after its
owner, this little shop in a
side street between Fuencarral
and Hortaleza specializes in
vintage fashions from the sixties
through to the seventies brought
over from England, France
and Scandinavia. The perfect
place to find retro party wear
or accessories. Lotta also has a
collection of her own designs.

Mercado Fuencarral

C/Fuencarral 45. Mon–Sat 10am–
10pm. Shopping mall catering
for the young fashion-conscious
crowd, filled with clubwear
shops, record stores, jewellers, a
café and even a tattoo parlour.

Pasajes

C/Genova 3 ⓦwww.pasajeslibros
.com. Mon–Fri 10am–2pm & 5–8pm,
Sat 10am–2pm. Interesting and
well-organized bookshop,
with extensive and up-to-date
English and foreign-language
sections, plus
language-
learning aids.

Reserva y Cata

C/Conde de Xiquena
13 ⓦwww
.reservaycata
.com. Mon 5–9pm,
Tues–Fri 11am–3pm

& 5–9pm, Sat 11am–3pm. Well-
informed staff at this friendly
specialist shop will help you
select from some of the best
new wines in the Iberian
peninsula.

La Tienda de Manola

C/Hortaleza 49. Mon–Fri 11am–
2.30pm, Sat 11am–2.30pm.
Marvellous little cheese shop
tucked between the street
fashion outlets that line this
road. You can pick up cheese
from all over Spain and if you
can't make up your mind the
friendly staff are happy to advise.
Sells wine too.

Tienda Olivarero

C/Mejia Lequerica 1 ⓦwww.pco.es
/usario/tienda.thm. Mon–Fri 10am–
2pm & 5–8pm, Sat 10am–2pm. This
outlet for an olive-growers' co-
operative has useful information
sheets to help you buy the best
olive oils from around Spain.

Cafés

Café Acuarela

C/Gravina 10. Daily 3pm–3am, Fri
& Sat till 4am. Comfy café, with
over-the-top Baroque decor
and great cocktails – the perfect
place for a quiet drink. Popular
with a mostly gay/lesbian
crowd.

Café Comercial

Glorieta de Bilbao 7. Daily 8am–1am,
Fri & Sat till 2am. A Madrileño

▼ CAFÉ COMERCIAL

institution and one of the city's most popular meeting points, this is a lovely traditional café full of mirrors, large tables and a cross section of Madrid society.

Café de Ruiz

C/Ruiz 11. Daily 11am–2am. Classic old-style Malasaña café and a great place to while away an afternoon. Discreet background music and good cakes are followed by cocktails in the evening.

Café Figueroa

C/Augusto Figueroa 17. Mon–Thurs 2.30pm–1am, Fri & Sat 2.30pm–2.30am, Sun 4pm–1am. Opened in the early 1980s, this is an established institution on the Madrileño gay scene, with regulars of all ages, a pool table upstairs and great parties during *Carnaval*.

Café la Palma

C/Palma 62 ⓦ www.cafelapalma.com. Daily 4pm–3am. Part traditional café, part arts and music venue, *Café La Palma* acts as a venue for a myriad of local artists ranging from singer-songwriters to storytellers. It also has popular DJ sessions on many evenings.

Restaurants

El 26 de Libertad

C/Libertad 26 ☎915 222 522. Mon 1–4pm, Tues–Thurs 1–4pm & 8pm–midnight, Fri & Sat 1–4pm & 9pm–midnight. Imaginative cuisine served up in an attentive but unfussy manner in this brightly decorated restaurant, popular with the Chueca locals. A very good €15 set menu is available at lunch times during the week, but not such a good deal in the evenings.

Annapurna

C/Zurbano 5 ☎913 198 716. Mon–Fri 1.30–4pm & 9pm–midnight, Sat 9pm–midnight. One of the better Indian restaurants in Madrid, especially if you go for the tandoori dishes or *thali*. Elegant surroundings and attentive service too, all for around €35 per person.

La Barraca

C/Reina 29 ☎915 327 154, ⓦ www .labarraca.es. Daily 1–4pm & 8.30pm–midnight. Step off the dingy street into this little piece of Valencia for some of the best *paella* in town. Service is attentive, the starters are excellent and there's a great lemon sorbet for dessert too. A three-course meal with wine costs around €35 a head.

Bazaar

C/Libertad 21 ☎915 233 905, ⓦ www .restaurantbazaar.com. Daily 1–4pm & 8.30–11.45pm. The fusion-style Mediterranean and Asian cuisine here has been a big hit on the Chueca scene. Lunch-time menu is just €9.40; evening meals under €20. The down side is the production-line-style

▲ LA BARRACA

service. No reservations, so arrive early to avoid waiting.

El Comunista (Tienda de Vinos)

C/Augusto Figueroa 35 ☎915 217 012. Mon–Sat 1–4.30pm & 9.30–11.45pm, Sun 9.30–11.45pm. Closed mid-Aug to mid-Sept. Long-established, popular *comedor* that has changed little since it was given its unofficial (but always used) name as a student haunt under Franco. The *sopa de ajo* (garlic soup) is particularly recommended. Expect to pay €4–8 for main courses.

Divina La Cocina

C/Colmenares 13 ☎915 313 765, ⓦwww.divinalacocina.com. Mon–Sun 1–4pm & 9pm–midnight (open till 1am on Sat & Sun). Fashionable, high quality restaurant tucked away in a little street close to Gran Vía. Its great value lunches (around €20) are a cut above most of its rivals, while there are some more expensive (around €20 for a main course), and even more tasty, options in the evening. Offerings include such delights as a red onion soup with crayfish tails, duck and ostrich hamburgers and superb cheesecakes for dessert.

La Gloria de Montera

C/Caballero de Gracia 10 ⓦwww.lagloriademontera.com. Daily 1–4.30pm & 8.30–11.45pm. Sister restaurant to *La Finca de Susana* (see p.84) with the same successful formula. Excellent value *menú* at €8.40 with imaginative, well-presented dishes on offer in a cool and airy setting. No reservations.

Gula Gula

Gran Vía 1 ☎915 228 764, ⓦwww.gulagula.net. Mon–Thurs 1–4.30pm & 9pm–2am, Fri & Sat 1–4.30pm & 9pm–3am. Spacious salad-bar-type restaurant that does a self-service buffet for around €20 (€9 at lunch time), and has live shows featuring drag queens and dancers every night (reservations for either 9pm or midnight). Popular for "hen nights" as well as with the gay crowd.

La Isla del Tesoro

C/Manuela Malasaña 3 ☎915 931 440. Mon–Sat 1.30–4pm & 9pm–midnight, Sun 9pm–midnight. The decor is tropical beach and the food cosmopolitan vegetarian at this good-value place. Service is not always up to standard however. The constantly changing *menú del día* is €9.50.

Momo

C/Libertad 8 ☎915 327 348. Daily 1–4pm & 9.30pm–midnight. Now re-located a few hundred metres from its former home, this well-established eatery on the Chueca scene is the place to go for a *menú del día* with a little bit extra. For €9 you get three courses, with some imaginative sauces, drinks and coffee. Unusually for Spain they also do a set dinner in the evening for €12. Very popular.

La Musa

C/Manuela Malasaña 18 ☎914 487 558. Daily 1.30–4.30pm & 8.30pm–midnight. It's easy to see why *La Musa* – a café, bar and restaurant all rolled into one – is such a firm favourite on the Malasaña scene. A variety of imaginative and tasty tapas, generous helpings, a strong wine list and chic decor are all part of the recipe for success. The only problem is the crowds.

Nina Madrid

C/Manuela Malasaña 10 ☎915 910 046. Mon–Fri 1.30–4.30pm & 8.30–11.30pm, Sat & Sun 12.30–5.30pm &

8.30–11.30pm. A stylish, modern restaurant serving a very good €11.30 *menú del día*, excellent weekend brunches (€18) and a tasty evening sampler menu for €28. Imaginative dishes such as duck with cauliflower and sea urchin sauce, and *croquetas* in satay sauce feature on the main menu but it is nowhere near as good value.

Ribeira do Miño

C/Santa Brígida 1 ☎915 219 854, ⓦ www.mariqueriaribeiradomino.com. Tues–Sun 1–5pm & 8pm–midnight. Great-value *marisquería*, serving a seafood platter for two at only €29; go for the slightly more expensive Galician white wine, Albariño, to accompany it. Efficient and friendly service. Very popular so make sure you book.

Salvador

C/Barbieri 12 ☎915 214 524. Mon–Sat 1.30–4pm & 9pm–midnight. Closed Aug. Bullfighting decor and excellent traditional favourites such as *rabo de toro* (bull's tail), *gallina en pepitoria* (chicken in almond sauce) and *arroz con leche* (rice pudding) in this Chueca classic. Lunch-time menu €20.

La Tasca Suprema

C/Argensola 7 ☎913 080 347. Mon–Sat 1.30–4pm. Closed Aug. Very popular, good-value, neighbourhood local, only open at lunch times and worth booking ahead for. Castilian home cooking done to perfection, including, on Monday and Thursday, *cocido* and excellent *pimientos de piquillo* (piquant red peppers).

Tapas bars

Albur

C/Manuela Malasaña 15. Daily

1–4.30pm & 8.30pm–12.30am. The decor is rustic and the food excellent here, but the service can be slow. The *champiñones en salsa verde* (mushrooms in a coriander sauce) and the *patatas albur* (potatoes with herbs and spices) are worth sampling. Lunch-time menu is around €9.

Baco y Beto

C/Pelayo 24. Mon–Fri 7.30pm–2am, Sat 1–4pm. Excellent creative tapas with great *tostas* and canapés. Try the courgette with melted brie and the *croquetas*. An excellent selection of wines too. The only disappointment is the limited opening hours.

El Bocaito

C/Libertad 6 ⓦ www.elbocaito .com. Mon–Fri 1–4.30pm & 8.30pm–midnight, Sat 8.30pm–midnight. Closed Aug. Watch the staff prepare the food in the kitchen as you munch away on a variety of delicious tapas. Look out for the *Luisito* (chilli, squid, mayonnaise and a secret sauce all topped with a prawn), the hottest canapé you're ever likely to encounter.

Santander

C/Augusto Figueroa 25. Mon–Sat 10.45am–4pm & 7.30–11pm. Closed Aug. Down-to-earth bar, famous for its vast range of tapas, including *tortillas* and quiche lorraine, as well as a huge variety of fresh home-made canapés at very reasonable prices.

Stop Madrid

C/Hortaleza 11. Mon–Sat noon–4pm & 7pm–midnight. An old-time corner bar with hams hanging from the windows and wine bottles lining the walls. Tapas consist largely of *jamón* and *chorizo*, with the "Canapé Stop" of ham and tomato doused in olive oil an excellent option. A very good tomato salad and a wide selection of wines.

Bars

Chicote

Gran Vía 12 ⊛ www.museo-chicote .com. Mon–Sat 5pm–1.30am. Opened back in 1931 by Perico Chicote, ex-barman at the *Ritz*, Sophia Loren, Frank Sinatra, Ava Gardner, Luis Buñuel, Orson Welles and the ubiquitous Hemingway have all passed through the doors. Unfortunately Chicote has lost much of its old-style charm as it has tried to keep up to date, though it's still worth a visit for nostalgia's sake.

Del Diego

C/Reina 12. Mon–Sat 9pm–3am. Closed Aug. An elegant New York-style cocktail bar set up by former *Chicote* waiter Fernando del Diego and now better than the original place. The expertly mixed cocktails are served up in a friendly, unhurried atmosphere. Superb margaritas, mojitos and manhattans, while the house special, a vodka-based Del Diego is a must.

Finnegans

Plaza de Las Salesas 9 ⊛ www .finnegansmadrid.com. Daily 1pm–2am. Large Irish bar with several rooms, complete with bar fittings and wooden floors brought over from the Emerald Isle. English-speaking staff and TV sports, plus a pub quiz on Monday nights.

Pepe Botella

C/San Andrés 12. 11am–2am. An old-style elegance still clings to this little bar which is perched

on the edge of the Plaza Dos de Mayo. Friendly staff, marble-topped tables, low-volume music and no fruit machine.

Taberna Ángel Sierra

C/Gravina 11, on Plaza Chueca. Daily noon–1am. One of the great bars in Madrid, where everyone drinks *vermút* accompanied by free, exquisite pickled anchovy tapas. *Raciones* are also available, though they're pretty pricey.

Clubs and disco-bares

Bogui

C/Barquillo 29. Mon–Sat 11.30pm–5am. Once the home of a well-known discobar called Kingston's, this club has been converted into a jazz venue holding live acts in the week. After 1am at the weekend the DJs take over and provide the music.

Liquid

C/Barquillo 8. Tues–Thurs & Sun 9pm–3am, Fri & Sat 9pm–3.30am. Smart and stylish gay bar, lined with video screens playing a selection of fashionable music to an equally fashionable clientele.

Oba-Oba

C/Jacometrezo 4. Mon–Sat 11pm–4am. €8. Long-established Latin club with a small dance floor and a fun atmosphere. It often has live Brazilian music accompanied by the obligatory *caipirinhas* and daiquris.

Ohm/Vektrum/Weekend at Bash

Plaza Callao 4 ⊛ www.tripfamily .com. Wed 11pm–6am, Thurs–Sat midnight–6am, Sun midnight–5am. Around €10. *Bash* is one of the major venues on the Madrid club scene. *OHM* is the main techno-house session on Friday and Saturday nights and is very popular with the gay crowd. There's funk and hip-hop on Wednesday, Thursday is electronic night with *Vektrum* and *Weekend* is the Sunday session for those who don't like Mondays.

Pachá

C/Barceló 11 ⓦ www.pacha-madrid. com. Wed–Sat midnight–5am. €12 with drink. An eternal survivor on the Madrid clubbing scene, Pachá runs an early session for under-age clubbers from 6.30–10.30pm on Fridays and Saturdays and then gets going with the real thing from midnight. House and techno plays on Saturdays; the music is more varied on other nights. It is open once a month on Sundays for a Mambo session.

▲ PACHÁ NIGHTCLUB

Tupperware

C/Corredera Alta de San Pablo 26. Daily 9pm–3.30am. The place to go for the latest on the indie scene, with a mix of grunge and classics from the punk era.

Salamanca and the Paseo de la Castellana

Exclusive Barrio de Salamanca was developed in the second half of the nineteenth century as an upmarket residential zone under the patronage of the Marquis of Salamanca. Today it's still home to Madrid's smartest apartments and designer emporiums, while the streets are populated by the chic clothes and sunglasses brigade, decked out in fur coats, Gucci and gold. Shopping aside, there's a scattering of sights here, including the pick of the city's smaller museums and Real Madrid's imposing Santiago Bernabéu stadium. Bordering Salamanca to the west is the multi-lane Paseo de la Castellana, peppered with corporate office blocks, where, in summer, the section north of Plaza de Colón is littered with trendy terrazas.

Plaza de Colón

Overlooking a busy crossroads and dominating the square in which they stand are a Neo-Gothic monument

▲ PLAZA DE COLÓN

to Christopher Columbus (Cristóbal Colón), given as a wedding gift to Alfonso XII, and an enormous Spanish flag. Directly behind are the Jardínes del Descubrimiento (Discovery Gardens), a small park containing three huge stone blocks representing Columbus's ships, the Niña, Pinta and Santa María. Below the plaza, underneath a cascading wall of water, is the 1970s **Centro Cultural de la Villa** (Tues–Sat 10am–9pm, Sat & Sun 10am–7pm), a venue for film, theatre and occasional exhibitions.

Biblioteca Nacional and Museo del Libro

Paseo de Recoletos 20 ⓦ www.bne .es. Tues–Sat 10am–9pm, Sun & hols 10am–2pm. Free. The National Library contains over six million volumes, including every work

Salamanca and the Paseo de la Castellana

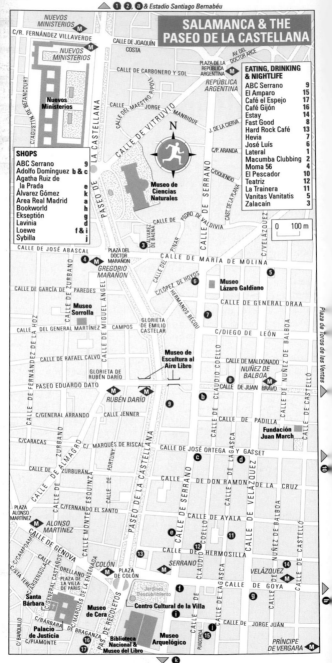

▲ ❶ ❷, ⓐ & Estadio Santiago Bernabéu

SALAMANCA & THE PASEO DE LA CASTELLANA

EATING, DRINKING & NIGHTLIFE

ABC Serrano	9
El Amparo	15
Café el Espejo	17
Café Gijón	16
Estay	14
Fast Good	8
Hard Rock Café	13
Hevia	7
José Luís	6
Lateral	1
Macumba Clubbing	2
Moma 56	4
El Pescador	10
Teatriz	12
La Trainera	11
Vanitas Vanitatis	5
Zalacaín	3

SHOPS

ABC Serrano	9
Adolfo Domínguez	b & c
Agatha Ruiz de la Prada	e
Álvarez Gómez	k
Area Real Madrid	a
Bookworld	h
Ekseptión	g
Lavinia	d
Loewe	f & i
Sybilla	j

0 — 100 m

Plaza de toros de las Ventas

published in Spain since 1716. The Museo del Libro (Book Museum) within displays a selection of the library's treasures, including Arab, Hebrew and Greek manuscripts, and has an interesting interactive exhibition on the development of written communication (in Spanish only).

Museo Arqueológico Nacional

C/Serrano 13 ⓦman.mcu.es. Tues–Sat 9.30am–8pm, Sun 9.30am–3pm. €3, free Sat after 2.30pm & all day Sun. The vast collections of the National Archeological Museum trace the cultural evolution of humankind. Most exhibits are from Spain and include striking **Celto-Iberian busts** known as *La Dama de Elche* and *La Dama de Baza*, as well as a wonderfully rich hoard of Visigothic treasures found at Toledo. Good coverage is also given to Roman, Egyptian, Greek and Islamic finds, but rooms are often closed for rearrangement.

In the gardens, a reconstruction of the prehistoric cave paintings of Altamira in Cantabria are the nearest you'll get to the real thing these days, since the caves themselves are now closed to the public.

Museo de Cera

Paseo de Recoletos 41 ⓦwww .museoceramadrid.com. Mon–Fri 10am–2.30pm & 4.30–8.30pm, Sat, Sun & hols 10am–8.30pm. €15 (€9 for 4–10 year olds). Over 450 different personalities – including a host of VIPs, heads of state and, of course, Real Madrid football stars – are displayed in this expensive and tacky museum, which is nevertheless popular with children. There's also a chamber of horrors and a film history of Spain (supplement charged).

Museo de Escultura al Aire Libre

Paseo de la Castellana 41 ⓦwww .munimadrid.es/museoairelibre. An innovative use of the space underneath the Juan Bravo flyover, the Open Air Sculpture Museum is made up of a haphazard collection, including work by Eduardo Chillida, Joan Miró and Julio González. The collection of cubes, walls, fountains and optical trickery appears to be most appreciated by the city's skateboard community.

Museo Sorolla

Paseo del General Martínez Campos 37 ⓦmuseosorolla.mcu.es. Tues & Thurs–Sat 9.30am–3pm, Wed 9.30am–6pm, Sun 10am–3pm. €2.40, free Sun. Part museum and part art gallery, this tribute to a single artist's life and work is one of Madrid's most underrated treasures. Situated in Joaquín Sorolla's former home – built in 1910 and donated to the nation by his widow in 1925 – it's a delightful oasis of peace and tranquillity, its cool and shady Andalusian-style courtyard and gardens decked out with statues, fountains, assorted plants and fruit trees.

▼ THE WOMAN OF ELCHE 400–350BC

PLACES Salamanca and the Paseo de la Castellana

▲ SOROLLA PAINTING

The ground floor has been kept largely intact, re-creating the authentic atmosphere of the artist's living and working areas. The upstairs rooms, originally the sleeping quarters, have been turned into a gallery, where sunlight, sea, intense colours, women and children dominate Sorolla's impressionistic paintings. On your way out in the Patio Andaluz, there's a small collection of his sketches and gouaches.

Museo Lázaro Galdiano

C/Serrano 122 ⓦ www.flg.es. Mon & Wed–Sun 10am–4.30pm. €4, free Sun. When businessman and publisher José Lázaro Galdiano died in 1947, he left his private collection – a vast treasure trove of paintings and *objets d'art* – to the state. Spread over the four floors of his former home, the collection contains jewellery, outstanding Spanish archeological pieces and some beautifully decorated thirteenth-century Limoges enamels. There's also an excellent selection of **European paintings** with works by Bosch, Rembrandt, Reynolds and Constable, plus Spanish artists including Zurbarán, Velázquez, El Greco and Goya. Other exhibits include several clocks and watches, many of them once owned by Carlos V.

Museo de Ciencias Naturales

C/José Gutiérrez Abascal 2 ⓦ www.mncn.csic.es. Tues–Fri 10am–6pm, Sat 10am–8pm (July & Aug 10am–3pm), Sun 10am–2.30pm. €2.40, free Sun. The Natural History Museum's displays are split between two buildings. One contains a fairly predictable collection of stuffed animals, skeletons and audiovisual displays on the evolution of life on earth, the other is home to some rather dull fossil and geological exhibits.

Nuevos Ministerios and the Zona Azca

Paseo de la Castellana. Nuevos Ministerios is a vast monolithic complex of government buildings, initiated during the Second Republic but completed under Franco. The bleak facade is broken only by the entrance to some gardens which are open to the public. A little further north is the conspicuously modern business quarter Zona Azca, once home to the city's tallest skyscraper – the 157-metre tall Torre Picasso (designed by Minori Yamasaki, also architect of the former Twin Towers in New York), although it is now dwarfed by the four new giant towers being built beyond Plaza Castilla.

Estadio Santiago Bernabéu

C/Concha Espina 1 ☎ 913 984 300,

tickets ☎902 324 324, ⓦwww
.realmadrid.com. Ticket office Mon–Fri
3–9pm (match days from 11am).
Tickets from €30 go on sale a week
before each match. Tour and trophy
exhibition Mon–Sat 10.30am–7pm,
Sun 10.30am–6.30pm; €10,
under-14s €7. The magnificent
80,000-seater Bernabéu stadium
provides a suitably imposing
home for the most glamorous
team in football, Real Madrid.
Venue of the 1982 World Cup
final, the stadium has witnessed
countless triumphs of "Los
blancos", who have notched
up 29 Spanish league titles and
nine European Cup triumphs in
their 105-year history. With the
departure of David Beckham,
Zinedine Zidane and Ronaldo,
the "Galactico" era is now
officially over, but Real retain
their cachet and an ample quota
of superstars. Tickets for big
games can be tricky to get hold
of, but the club run a telephone
and Internet booking service.
If using the phone service the
best technique when calling
is to remain silent when asked
questions by the automated
system; you then get passed to
an operator (most of whom
speak English) who provides
tickets more efficiently. If you
want to book over the Internet
look at the section entitled
"proximo partido" on the club's
web page.

You can catch a glimpse of
the hallowed turf on the overpriced stadium tour (tickets on
sale Puerta 7, entrance Puerta
20) during which you visit the
changing rooms, walk around
the edge of the pitch and sit in
the VIP box before heading to
the trophy room with its endless
cabinets of gleaming silverware.
Note that tour schedules are
disrupted on match days and
when the team is training,
so it's worth checking before
you go. The stadium also has a
reasonably priced café (*Realcafé*)
and a more expensive restaurant
(*Puerta 57*) both open to the
public and affording views over
the pitch (though they are not
open during games).

Plaza Castilla

The Paseo de la Castellana ends
with a flourish at Plaza Castilla
with the dramatic leaning
towers of the Puerta de Europa.
Construction of the smoked-
glass office blocks was financed
by the Kuwait Investment

▼ ESTADIO SANTIAGO BERNABÉU

▲ PUERTO EUROPA AT PLAZA CASTILLA

Office (KIO) until the collapse of its Spanish subsidiary in one of the country's biggest-ever bankruptcies. The towers stood unfinished for several years until the powerful local bank Caja Madrid came to the rescue. All in all they provide a pretty fitting testimony to the uncontrolled property speculation of the 1980s.

Over the next 20 years the plan is to extend the Castellana another 3.5km northwards as part of the local authority's ambitious attempt to convert the area into one of Europe's major business centres. Four giant skyscrapers are already under construction on Real Madrid's former training ground, the result of a controversial deal that allowed the club to solve many of its financial problems. The two tallest towers, one of which is designed by Norman Foster, will soar some 250 metres into the sky.

Plaza de Toros de Las Ventas

C/Alcalá 237 ☎ 913 562 200, ⓦ www .las-ventas.com. Box office March–Oct Thurs–Sun 10am–2pm & 5–8pm; BBVA ticket line ☎ 902 150 025, ⓦ www.taquilatoros.com and from authorized agents in booths along c/Victoria near Sol. €5–110. Situated on the easternmost tip of the Barrio de Salamanca, Madrid's 23,000-capacity, Neo-Mudéjar bullring, Las Ventas, is the most illustrious in the world. The season lasts from March to October and *corridas* (bullfights) are held every Sunday at 7pm and every day during the three main *ferias* (*fairs*): La Comunidad (early May), San Isidro (mid-May to June) and Otoño (late Sept to Oct). Tickets go on sale at the ring a couple of days in advance, though many are already allocated to season-ticket holders. The cheapest seats are *gradas*, the highest rows at the back, from where you can see everything that happens without too much of the detail; the front rows are known as the *barreras*. Seats are also divided into *sol* (sun), *sombra* (shade) and *sol y sombra* (shaded after a while), with *sombra* seats the most expensive.

There's a taurine **museum** attached to the bullring (March–Oct Tues–Fri 9.30am–2.30pm, Sun & fight days 10am–1pm; Nov–Feb Mon–Fri 9.30am–2pm; free) with an intriguing if rather anarchic collection of bullfighting memorabilia including stunning *trajes de luces*, the beautifully decorated suits worn by the *toreros*.

Shops

ABC Serrano

Paseo de la Castellana 34 and c/ Serrano 61 ⓦ www.abcserrano.com. Mon–Sat 10am–8pm. Upmarket shopping mall housed in the beautiful former headquarters of the *ABC* newspaper. There are fashion and household outlets, as well as a couple of bars and restaurants.

Adolfo Domínguez

C/Serrano 18 & 96 ⓦwww
.adolfo-dominguez.com. Mon–Sat
10am–8.30pm. C/José Ortega y Gasset
4. Mon–Sat 10am–2pm & 5–8.30pm.
Domínguez's classic modern Spanish designs – a wide range of colours and free lines – are quite pricey but he does have a cheaper *Basico* range. The branch at Serrano 18 stocks the complete range of clothes, whereas the Ortega y Gasset branch specializes in accessories.

Agatha Ruiz de la Prada

C/Serrano 27 ⓦwww
.agatharuizdelaprada.com. Mon–Sat
10am–8.30pm. *Movida*-era designer who shows and sells her gaudily coloured clothes and accessories at this outlet. There's a children's line, stationery and household goods too.

Álvarez Gómez

C/Serrano 14 ⓦwww.halvarezgomez
.com. Mon–Sat 10am–2pm &
5–8.30pm. Álvarez Gómez has been making the same perfumes in the same bottles for over a hundred years, with fragrances – carnation, rose and violet – that are as simple as they come. The elegant shop, complete with chandeliers, also sells stylish toilet bags, hats and umbrellas.

Area Real Madrid

C/Concha Espina 1 and Bernabéu
Stadium. Mon–Sat 10am–8pm,
Sun 11am–8pm (c/Concha Espina
branch). Club store where you can pick up replica shirts of the star players and all manner of – expensive – souvenirs related to the club's history.

Bookworld

C/Goya 56 ⓦwww.bookworldespana
.com. Mon–Sat 10am–8pm. Newly opened English bookshop selling an extensive range of fiction, general interest, travel, reference and children's books.

Ekseptión

C/Velázquez 28 ⓦwww.eks-madrid
.tv. Mon–Sat 10.30am–2.30pm &
5–8.30pm. A dramatic catwalk bathed in spotlights leads into this shop selling some of the most expensive women's clothes in Madrid. Next door are younger, more casual clothes in the Eks shop for both men and women. There's also a branch selling discount last-season fashions at half price at Avda Concha Espina 14 (Mon–Sat 11.30am–8pm).

Lavinia

C/José Ortega y Gasset 16 ⓦwww
.lavinia.es. Mon–Sat 10.30am–9pm. A massive wine shop with a great

▼ ABC SERRANO MALL

PLACES

Salamanca and the Paseo de la Castellana

selection from Spain and the rest of the world. The perfect place to get that Ribera del Duero, Albariño or Rueda that you wanted to take home.

Loewe

C/Serrano 26 & 34 ⓦ www.loewe.es. 9.30am–8.30pm. Luxury leather goods for men and women – including shoes, belts and bags – from this high-priced Spanish designer label.

Sybilla

C/Jorge Juan 12. Mon–Sat 10am–2pm & 4.30–8.30pm. Top designer Sybilla broke through in the 1980s and remains at the forefront of the women's fashion scene in Spain – with prices to match. Also does a jewellery line and accessories for the home. If shopping gets too tiring, there are armchairs and sofas to collapse into.

Cafés

Café el Espejo

Paseo de Recoletos 31 ⓦ www .restauranteelespejo.com. Daily 8am–1am. Opened in 1978, but you wouldn't guess it from the antiquated decor – mirrors, gilt and a wonderful, extravagant glass pavilion, plus a leafy outside *terraza*. An ideal spot to buy a coffee and watch the world go by. There is a smoke-free restaurant (a rarity in Spain) in the main café.

Café Gijón

Paseo de Recoletos 21. Daily 8am–1.30am. Famous literary café dating from 1888, decked out in Cuban mahogany and mirrors. A centre of the *Movida* in the 1980s, it still hosts regular artistic *tertulias* (discussion groups). There's a cellar restaurant, a very pleasant summer *terraza* and a set menu at lunch time.

Restaurants

El Amparo

Callejón Puigcerdá 8 ☎ 914 316 456. Mon–Fri 1.30–3.30pm & 9–11.30pm, Sat 9–11.30pm. Critics rate this designer restaurant among the top five in Madrid – and you'll need to book a couple of weeks ahead to get a table. If you strike

▲ CAFÉ EL ESPEJO

it lucky, the rewards are faultless Basque cooking, top-class ingredients and fantastic desserts. Mains cost €25–30 so expect to pay at least €60 a head.

▲ ZALACAÍN RESTAURANT

Estay

C/Hermosilla 46 ☎915 780 470, ⓦwww .estayrestaurante.com. Mon–Sat 1–4pm & 8pm–midnight. Basque-style cuisine in miniature (canapés and mini casseroles) in this pleasant and roomy Salamanca restaurant. A great range of *pintxos*, including *jamón* with roquefort cheese, langoustine vol-au-vents and a fine wine list too. A meal will cost €25-30.

Fast Good

C/Juan Bravo 3 ⓦwww.fast-good.com. Daily noon–midnight. Brainchild of Catalan chef Ferrán Adrià, the idea is to provide upmarket, high-quality fast food. Healthy hamburgers, panini, salads and sandwiches are all on offer. There are other branches in the barrio at c/Orense 11 and c/Padre Damian 23 below the NH Eurobuilding hotel.

Hard Rock Café

Paseo de la Castellana 2 ☎914 364 340. Daily 12.30pm–2am. A children's favourite, with its tried-and-tested formula of rock memorabilia, Tex-Mex and burgers at under €20 a head. The best thing about it is the summer *terraza* overlooking Plaza Colón.

El Pescador

C/José Ortega y Gasset 75 ☎914 021 290. Mon–Sat 1–4pm & 9pm–midnight. Closed Aug. One of the city's top seafood restaurants,

with specials flown in from the Atlantic each morning. Prices are high (around €55 per head), but you'll rarely experience better quality seafood than this.

La Trainera

C/Lagasca 60 ☎915 768 035, ⓦwww.latrainera.es. Mon–Sat 1–4pm & 8pm–midnight. Closed Aug. Another high-quality seafood place, popular with politicians and businessmen, with prices to match (bank on €40–50 a head). Seafood platters, very fresh fish and an excellent selection of wines.

Zalacaín

C/Álvarez de Baena 4 ☎915 614 840. Mon–Fri 1.15–4pm & 9pm–midnight, Sat 9pm–midnight. Closed Aug. A luxurious setting for one of the best – and most expensive – restaurants in town. Basque-style cooking from master chef Benjamín Urdaín, but you pay for the pleasure with a meal costing around €95 per person. Male customers must wear jacket and tie.

Tapas bars

Hevia

C/Serrano 118. Mon–Sat 9am–1.30am. Plush venue and clientele for pricey but excellent tapas and canapés – the hot Camembert is delicious, as is the *surtido de ahumados* (selection of smoked fish).

José Luís

C/Serrano 89. Mon–Sat 9am–1am, Sun noon–11pm. The best of this chain of smart bar/restaurants, established by a Basque in the late 1950s. It serves dainty and delicious sandwiches, along with canapés of crab, black pudding and steak, but the bill quickly mounts up if you're not careful.

Lateral

Paseo de la Castellana 132. Daily 10am–midnight. A swish tapas bar serving a good variety of classic dishes such as *croquetas* and *pimientos rellenos* (stuffed peppers) with a modern twist. This one is close to the Bernabéu and gets crowded on match days but there are other branches at c/Velázquez 57 and c/Fuencarral 43. In summer there is a lively *terraza* outside.

Bars

ABC Serrano

Paseo de la Castellana 34. Popular summer rooftop terrace on the fourth floor of this rather exclusive Salamanca shopping mall overlooking the Castellana.

Teatriz

C/Hermosilla 15. Bar 9pm–3am, restaurant 1.30–4.30pm & 9pm–1am; closed Sat lunch, Sun & Aug. This former theatre, redesigned by Catalan designer Mariscal and Philippe Starck, is as elegant

a club/bar/restaurant as any in Europe. There are bars on the main theatre levels, while down in the basement there's a library-like area and small disco. Drinks are pretty pricey but there's no entrance charge.

Clubs and discobares

Macumba Clubbing

Estación de Chamartín ☎902 499 994, ⓦ www.spaceofsound.net. Elite Noche: Sat midnight–6am. Space of Sound: Sun 9am–6pm. €15 including first drink. Guest DJs from London's *Ministry of Sound* come for the Saturday Elite Noche all-nighter and if you just can't stop till you get enough, the Space of Sound "after hours" club allows you to strut your stuff through Sunday too.

Moma 56

C/José Abasca ⓦ www.moma56 .com. Wed–Sun midnight–6am. Around €15. An exclusive New York-style club, popular with *pijos* (rich kids) and the upmarket glamour crowd. Also inside are the *Asia Lounge* restaurant and a bar serving cocktails and light Mediterranean fusion food.

Vanitas Vanitatis

C/Velázquez 128. Mon–Thurs & Sun 8.30pm–3am, Fri & Sat 10pm–5am. A fashionable nightspot that has been a popular stop-off on the Salamanca scene for the best part of a decade. Posey, thirty-something clientele and strict door policy.

Plaza de España and beyond

Largely constructed in the Franco era and dominated by two early Spanish skyscrapers, the Plaza de España provides an imposing full stop to Gran Vía and a breathing space from the densely packed streets to the east. Beyond the square lies a mixture of aristocratic suburbia, university campus and parkland, distinguished by the green swathes of Parque del Oeste and Casa de Campo. Sights include the eclectic collections of the Museo Cerralbo, the fascinating Museo de América, the Ermita de San Antonio de la Florida, with its stunning Goya frescoes and, further out, the pleasant royal residence of El Pardo. Meanwhile, the spacious terrazas along Paseo del Pintor Rosales provide ample opportunity for refreshment.

Plaza de España

The Plaza de España was the Spanish dictator Franco's attempt to portray Spain as a dynamic, modern country. The gargantuan apartment complex of the **Edificio de España**, which heads the square, looks like it was transplanted from

▲ MONUMENT OF DON QUIXOTE, PLAZA DE ESPAÑA

1920s New York, but was in fact completed in 1953. Four years later, the 32-storey **Torre de Madrid** took over for some time as the tallest building in Spain. Together they tower over an elaborate **monument to Cervantes** in the middle of the square, set by an uninspiring pool. The plaza itself can be a little seedy at night, although it does play host to occasional festivities and an interesting craft fair during the fiesta of San Isidro (on or around May 15).

Museo de Cerralbo

C/Ventura Rodríguez 17
ⓦ museocerralbo.mcu.es. Tues–Sat 9.30am–3pm, Sun & hols 10am–3pm; July & Aug Tues–Sat 9.30am–2pm, Sun & hols 11am–2pm. Free guided visits Wed 11am & Sat noon. €2.40, free Wed & Sun. Reactionary politician, poet, traveller and archeologist, the seventeenth Marqués de Cerralbo endowed his elegant nineteenth-century mansion with a substantial collection of

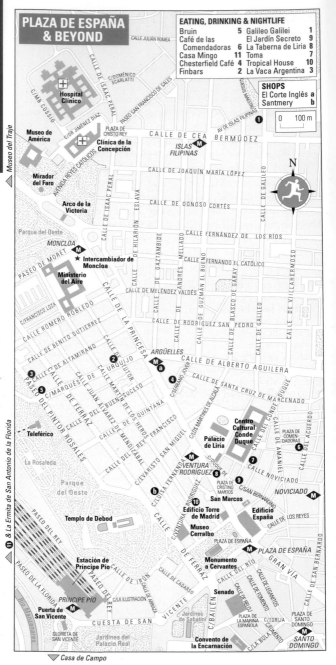

PLAZA DE ESPAÑA & BEYOND

EATING, DRINKING & NIGHTLIFE

Bruin	5	Galileo Galilei	1
Café de las Comendadoras	6	El Jardín Secreto	9
Casa Mingo	11	La Taberna de Liria	8
Chesterfield Café	4	Toma	7
Finbars	2	Tropical House	10
		La Vaca Argentina	3

SHOPS

El Corte Inglés	a
Santmery	b

0   100 m

paintings, furniture and armour. Bequeathed to the state on his death, the house opened as a museum in 1962 and the cluttered nature of the exhibits is partly explained by the fact that the marqués's will stipulated that objects should be displayed exactly as he had arranged them. The highlight is a fabulous over-the-top mirrored ballroom with a Tiepolo-inspired fresco, golden stucco work and marbled decoration.

Centro Cultural Conde Duque

C/Conde Duque 9–11 ⓦwww .munimadrid.es/condeduque. Summer: Tues–Sat 10am–2pm & 6–9pm, Sun 10.30am–2pm; winter: Tues–Sat 10am–9pm, Sun 11am–2.30pm. Free. Constructed in the early eighteenth century, this former barracks of the royal guard has been converted into a dynamic cultural centre, housing the city's collection of contemporary art and hosting a variety of temporary exhibitions. It also stages an excellent series of concerts, plays and dance as part of the local council's *Veranos de la Villa* season in the summer.

Plaza de Comendadoras

Bordered by a variety of interesting craft shops, bars and cafés, this tranquil square is named after the convent that occupies one side of it. The convent is run by nuns from the military order of Santiago and the attached church is decked out with banners celebrating the victories of the order's knights. A large painting of their patron, St James the Moor-slayer, hangs over the high altar. The plaza itself comes alive in the summer months when the *terrazas* open and locals gather for a chat and a drink.

El Ministerio del Aire

The Air Ministry is another product of the post–Civil War Francoist building boom. Work on the mammoth edifice began in 1942, and even the Third Reich's architect, Albert Speer, was consulted. However, with the defeat of the Nazis, plans were soon changed and a Habsburg-style structure was built instead – nicknamed the "Monasterio" del Aire because of its similarity to El Escorial. The neighbouring Arco de la Victoria was constructed in 1956 to commemorate the Nationalist military triumph in the Civil War.

Mirador del Faro

May to mid-Oct Tues–Sun 10am–2pm & 5pm–dusk; mid-Oct to May Tues–Fri 10am–2pm & 5–7pm, Sat & Sun 10am –6pm. €1. At 92m high,

▼ CENTRO CULTURAL CONDE DUQUE

▲ MIRADOR DEL FARO

this futuristic viewing tower provides stunning views over the city and to the mountains beyond. It's unfortunate then that there are no explanation panels to identify what you're seeing.

Museo de América

Avda de los Reyes Católicos 6. ⓦwww .museodeamerica.mcu.es. Tues–Sat 9.30am–3pm, Sun 10am–3pm. €3, free Sun. This fabulous collection of pre-Columbian American art and artefacts includes objects brought back at the time of the Spanish Conquest, as well as more recent acquisitions and donations. The layout is thematic, with sections on geography, history, social organization, religion and communication. The Aztec, Maya and Inca civilizations are well represented and exhibits include: the Madrid Codex, one of only three surviving hieroglyphic manuscripts depicting everyday Maya life; the Tudela Codex, including indigenous paintings describing the events of the Spanish Conquest; and the Quimbayas Treasure, a breathtaking collection of gold objects from a funeral treasure of the Colombian Quimbaya culture, dated 900–600 BC.

Museo del Traje

Avda de Juan de Herrera 2. ⓦwww .museodeltraje.mcu.es. Tues–Sat 9.30am–7pm, Sun & hols 10am–3pm. €3, free under-18s, Sat after 2.30pm and all day Sun. A fascinating excursion through the history of clothes and costume. Exhibits

▲ QUIMBAYAS TREASURE, MUSEO DE AMÉRICA

include garments from a royal tomb dating back to the thirteenth century, some stunning eighteenth-century ballgowns and a selection of Spanish regional costumes as well as shoes, jewellery and underwear. Modern Spanish and international designers are also featured, with a Paco Rabane mini-skirt and elegant shoes from Pedro del Hierro.

▲ MUSEO DEL TRAJE

Parque del Oeste

Featuring a pleasant stream, assorted statues and shady walks, this delightful park offers a welcome respite from the busy streets of the capital. In summer there are numerous *terrazas* overlooking it on Paseo del Pintor Rosales. The beautiful rose garden – in c/Rosaleda – is at its most fragrant in May and June, while further down the hill is a small cemetery where the 43 Spaniards executed by occupying French troops on May 3, 1808 – and immortalized by Goya in his famous painting in the Prado – lie buried.

Templo de Debod

Ferraz 1 ⓦwww.munimadrid .es/templodebod/. April– Sept Tues–Fri 10am–2pm & 6–8pm, Sat & Sun 10am–2pm; Oct–March Tues–Fri 9.45am–1.45pm & 4.15–6.15pm, Sat & Sun 10am–2pm. Free. A fourth-century BC Egyptian temple in the middle of Madrid may seem an incongruous sight. It's here, however, as a thank you from the Egyptian government for Spanish help in salvaging archeological sites threatened by the construction of the Aswan High Dam. Reconstructed here stone by stone in 1968, it has a multimedia exhibition on the culture of Ancient Egypt inside. Archeologists have called for it to be enclosed and insulated from the open air as pollution is taking a heavy toll on the stone.

El Teleférico

Paseo del Pintor Rosales ⓦwww .teleferico.com/madrid. April–Sept Mon–Fri noon–early eve (exact times vary), Sat & Sun noon–around 8pm; Oct–March Sat, Sun & hols noon–dusk. €3.25 single, €4.65 return. Running from the edge of the Parque del Oeste is the Teleférico, a cable car that shuttles its passengers high over the Manzanares River to a

▲ TEMPLO DE DEBOD

restaurant/bar in the middle of Casa de Campo (see adjacent). The round trip offers some fine views of the park, the Palacio Real, the Almudena Cathedral and the city skyline.

La Ermita de San Antonio de la Florida

Paseo de la Florida 5 Ⓦ www .munimadrid.es/ermita. Tues–Fri 9.30am–8pm, Sat & Sun 10am–2pm; July 13–23 closed pm. Free. Built on a Greek-cross plan between 1792 and 1798, this little church is the burial site of Goya and also features some outstanding frescoes by him. Those in the recently restored dome depict St Anthony of Padua resurrecting a dead man to give evidence in favour of a prisoner (the saint's father) unjustly accused of murder. The *ermita* also houses the artist's mausoleum, although his head was stolen by phrenologists for examination in the nineteenth century.

▼ CASA CAMPO LAKE

The mirror-image chapel on the other side of the road was built in 1925 for parish services so that the original could become a museum. On St Anthony's Day (June 13) girls queue at the church to ask the saint for a boyfriend; if pins dropped into the holy water then stick to their hands, their wish will be granted.

Casa de Campo

The Casa de Campo, an enormous expanse of heath and scrub, is in parts surprisingly wild for a place so easily accessible from the city. Founded by Felipe II in the mid-sixteenth century as a royal hunting estate, it was only opened to the public in 1931 and soon after acted as a base for Franco's forces to shell the city. Large sections have been tamed for conventional pastimes and there are picnic tables and café/bars throughout the park, the ones by the lake providing fine views of the city. There are also mountain-bike trails, a jogging track, an open-air swimming pool (June–Sept daily 10.30am–8pm; €4), tennis courts, and rowing boats for rent on the lake, all near Metro Lago. The park is best avoided after dark as many of its roads are frequented by prostitutes.

Zoo-Aquarium

Casa de Campo ☎ 917 119 950, Ⓦ www.zoomadrid.com. Daily 11am–dusk. €15.90, 3–7 year-olds €12.90, under-3s free. Laid out in sections corresponding to the five continents, Madrid's zoo, on the southwestern edge of Casa de Campo, provides decent enclosures and plenty of space for over 2000 different species. When you've had your fill of big cats, koalas and venomous snakes, you can check out the aquarium, dolphinarium, children's zoo or bird show. Boats can be rented and there are mini train tours too.

Parque de Atracciones

Casa de Campo ☎915 268 030 or ☎914 632 900, Ⓦwww .parquedeatracciones.es. April–Sept most days noon–midnight (consult website); Oct–March weekends and hols noon–7pm. Access only €8.20; entry with unlimited access to rides (Calco Adulto) €26, 3–6 year-olds €16. This is Madrid's most popular theme park, where highlights include the new Tarantula rollercoaster, the 63-metre vertical drop, La Lanzadera, the stomach-churning La Máquina, the whitewater raft ride, Los Rápidos, and the haunted house, El Viejo Caserón. Spanish acts perform in the open-air auditorium in the summer and there are frequent parades too, plus plenty of burger/pizza places to replace lost stomach contents.

Hipódromo de la Zarzuela

Carretera La Coruña km 8 Ⓦwww .hipodromodelazarzuela.es. €9 for a general entry. There is a free bus that goes from Paseo de Moret next to the Intercambiador in Moncloa. The horse racing track just out of the city on the A Coruña road has reopened after a decade of neglect and holds races every Sunday in the spring and autumn. The unstuffy atmosphere and a beautiful setting make this a fun day out for all the family.

El Pardo

C/Manuel Alonso Ⓦwww .patrimonionacional.es. April–Sept Mon–Sat 10.30am–5.45pm, Sun 9.30am–1.30pm; Oct–March Mon–Sat 10.30am-4.45pm, Sun 10am–1.30pm; closed for official visits. Guided tours €5, free Wed for EU citizens. Buses from Moncloa (daily 6.30am–midnight; every 10–15min; 25min) make the nine-kilometre journey northwest of central Madrid to Franco's former principal residence at El Pardo. A garrison still remains at the town, where most of the Generalíssimo's staff were based, but the place is now a popular excursion for Madrileños, who come here for long lunches at the excellent *terraza* restaurants.

The tourist focus is the **Palacio del Pardo**, rebuilt by the Bourbons on the site of the hunting lodge of Carlos I and still used by visiting heads of state. Behind the imposing but blandly symmetrical facade, the interior houses the chapel where Franco prayed, and the theatre where he used to censor films. On display are a number of mementos of the dictator, including his desk, a portrait of Isabel la Católica and an excellent collection of tapestries. Tickets to the palace are also valid for the neighbouring pavilion, the Casita del Príncipe.

Shops

Santmery

C/Juan Álvarez Mendizábal 27. Mon–Fri 9.30am–3pm & 5.30–10pm, Sat 9.30am–3pm. Fascinating wine shop that also doubles as a bar and delicatessen. You can sample some of the wines by the glass, while more exclusive ones have to be bought by the bottle. Try some of the top-quality cheese and ham too, or even the house speciality *mousse de cabrales a la sidra* (blue cheese and cider paté).

Plaza de España and beyond

El Corte Inglés

C/Princesa 41 & 56. Mon–Sat 10am–10pm. One of many branches of Spain's biggest and most popular department store. It stocks everything from souvenirs and gift items to clothes and electrical goods. Prices are on the high side, but quality is usually very good.

Cafés

Bruin

Paseo Pintor Rosales 48. Daily noon–1am. Old-fashioned ice-cream parlour – serving 35 different varieties – that makes a good stop-off point before heading into nearby Parque del Oeste. Iced drinks are also on sale and there's a very pleasant summer terrace too.

Café de las Comendadoras

Plaza de las Comendadoras 1. Daily: winter 6pm–1.30am; summer noon–1.30am. Relaxing café with a buzzing summer *terraza*, situated on one of the city's nicest squares. There are two other decent café-bars alongside if this one is too crowded.

Restaurants

Casa Mingo

Paseo de la Florida 34 ☏915 477 918. Daily 11am–midnight. Closed Aug. Noisy, crowded and reasonably priced Asturian chicken-and-cider house. Tables are like gold dust, so loiter with your bottle of *sidra* in hand. The spit-roast chicken is practically compulsory, though the *chorizo* cooked in cider and *cabrales* (blue cheese) is also very good. Well worth the €18 a head.

La Taberna de Liria

C/Duque de Liria 9 ☏915 414 519. Mon–Fri 1.30–3.30pm & 9.30–11.30pm, Sat 9.15–11.30pm. Closed Aug. Excellent, but quiet restaurant serving Mediterranean-style dishes with a French touch. Great fish, inventive salads and delicious desserts, though on the pricey side at around €45–50 a head.

Toma

C/Conde Duque 14 ☏915 474 996. Tues–Sat 9pm–12.30am. Intimate little restaurant with just a handful of tables in a bright red room, where husband and wife team Paul and Angela serve up a constantly changing menu with a creative twist. Booking is essential and budget on €25–30 a head.

La Vaca Argentina

Paseo del Pintor Rosales 52 ☏915 596 605, ⊛www.lavacaargentina.net. Daily 1–5pm & 9pm–midnight. One of a chain of restaurants serving Argentine-style grilled steaks (*churrasco*). This branch has good views of the Parque del Oeste from its summer terrace, but service can be slow. Average cost is around €25.

Bars

El Jardín Secreto

C/Conde Duque 2. Mon–Thurs 5.30pm–midnight, Fri & Sat 6pm–2am. Cosy, dimly lit bar on the corner of a tiny plaza close to Plaza de España serving reasonably priced drinks and cocktails. Service is friendly and the atmosphere reassuringly unhurried.

Finbars

C/Marqués de Urquijo 10. Mon–Fri 10.30am–1.30am, Sat & Sun noon–2am. Satellite sports broadcasts

▲ SALSA DANCING AT TROPICAL HOUSE

and Guinness in this friendly Irish bar on an attractive street close to the Parque del Oeste.

Clubs and discobares

Chesterfield Café

C/Serrano Jover 5 ⓦwww .chesterlounge.com. Daily 1.30pm–3am. This American-style club/restaurant serves Tex-Mex food and cocktails and hosts international parties and regular concerts (for which you pay).

Galileo Galilei

C/Galileo 100 ⓦwww.salagalileogalilei .com. Daily 6pm–4.30am. €4–10. Bar, concert venue and disco rolled into one. Latin music is regularly on offer, along with cabaret and flamenco.

Tropical House

C/Martín de los Heros 14. Wed, Thurs & Sun 11pm–5am, Fri & Sat 11.30pm–6am. One of the biggest and best salsa venues in the city. Dance the night away to tropical vibes or simply enjoy the spectacle as you watch the experts.

El Escorial and Valle de los Caídos

Fifty kilometres northwest of Madrid, in the foothills of the Guadarrama mountains, lies one of Spain's most visited sights – Felipe II's immense monastery-palace complex of El Escorial. Built between 1563 and 1584 by Juan Bautista de Toledo and Juan de Herrera, the monk-like Felipe planned the austere structure as monastery, mausoleum and palace. The result dominates the surrounding town and provides an unprecedented insight into the mindset of Spain's greatest king.

Some 9km further north and easily visited from El Escorial, El Valle de los Caídos (The Valley of the Fallen) is an equally megalomaniacal, yet far more chilling monument: an underground basilica hewn under Franco's orders, allegedly to commemorate the Civil War dead of both sides, though in reality a memorial to the Generalíssimo and his regime.

EL Escorial

El Escorial was the largest Spanish building of the Renaissance, built to celebrate a victory over the French in 1557 and divided into different sections for secular and religious use. Linking the two zones is the **Biblioteca** (Library), a splendid hall with vivid, multicoloured frescoes by Tibaldi. The library's collections include Santa Teresa's personal diary, some gorgeously executed

Visiting El Escorial

There are around 25 **trains** a day to El Escorial from Madrid (5.45am–11.30pm from Atocha, calling at Chamartín), or **buses** #661 and #664 from the *intercambiador* at Moncloa run every fifteen minutes on weekdays and hourly at weekends. **Opening hours** of the complex are Tues–Sun: April–Sept 10am–6pm; Oct–March 10am–5pm. Tickets cost €7 for a visit of the key rooms, €8 for a more comprehensive tour, €9 for a guided visit; combined ticket with El Valle de los Caídos €8.50 non-guided, €10 guided; free Wed for EU citizens. Visit ⓦwww.patrimonionacional.es for up-to-date information on both. The helpful **oficina de turismo** (Mon–Fri 10am–6pm, Fri–Sun 10am–7pm; ☏918 905 313, ⓦwww.sanlorenzoturismo.org) is at c/Grimaldi 4.

To visit **El Valle de los Caídos** from El Escorial, there's a local bus run by Herranz (#660), which starts from their office in Plaza de la Virgen de Gracía, just north of the visitors' entrance to the monastery. The bus runs from El Escorial at 3.15pm, returning at 5.30pm (Tues–Sun; €8 return including entrance to the monument).

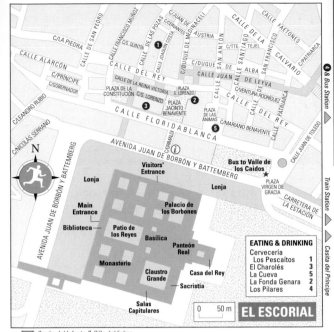

& Bus Station ►

Train Station ►

Casita del Príncipe ►

EATING & DRINKING

Cervecería Los Pescaítos	1
El Charolés	3
La Cueva	5
La Fonda Genara	2
Los Pilares	4

EL ESCORIAL

0   50 m

▽ Casita del Infanta & Silla del Felipe

Arabic manuscripts and a Florentine planetarium of 1572 demonstrating the movement of the planets. Beyond is the Patio de los Reyes, named after the six statues of the kings of Israel which adorn the facade of the Basílica, on the far side of the courtyard.

The enormous, cold, dark interior of the **Basílica** contains over forty altars, designed to allow simultaneous Masses to be held. Behind the main altar lies some of Felipe's mammoth collection of saintly relics, including six whole bodies, over sixty heads and hundreds of bone fragments set in fabulously expensive caskets.

You can also wander round some of El Escorial's courtyards including the Claustro Grande with its Tibaldi frescoes

depicting the life of the Virgin, and the secluded gardens of the Patio de los Evangelistas that lie within.

Many of the monastery's religious treasures are contained in the **Sacristía** and **Salas Capitulares** (Chapter Houses) and include paintings by Titian, Velázquez and José Ribera. Below these rooms is the Panteón Real, where past Spanish monarchs lie in their gilded marble tombs. The royal children are laid in the Panteón de los Infantes and there's also a babies' tomb with room for sixty infants.

What remains of El Escorial's art collection – works by Bosch, Dürer, Titian, Zurbarán, among others that escaped transfer to the Prado – is kept in the elegant Museos Nuevos. Don't

▲ EL ESCORIAL

miss the Sala de Batallas, a long gallery lined with an epic series of paintings depicting important imperial battles. Finally, there are the treasure-crammed *Salones Reales* (Royal Apartments), containing the austere quarters of Felipe II, with the chair that supported his gouty leg and the deathbed from which he was able to contemplate the high altar of the Basílica.

Casita del Príncipe and Casita del Infante

Casita del Principe: April–June Sat, Sun & hols 10am–7pm; July–Sept Tues–Sun 10am–7pm; €3.60; tours only, every 30min; reservations ☎918 905 903. Casita del Infante: April–June Sat, Sun & hols 10am–1pm & 4–6.30pm; July–Sept Tues-Sun 10am–1pm & 4–6.30pm; €3.40, free Wed for EU citizens.

The outlying buildings of the complex, the Casita del Príncipe (aka Casita de Abajo) and the Casita del Infante (aka Casita de Arriba), are two eighteenth-century royal lodges both full of decorative riches, and built by Juan de Villanueva, Spain's most accomplished Neoclassical architect. Their greatest appeal, however, lies in wandering through their delightful formal gardens.

La Silla de Felipe

Around 3km out of town is the Silla de Felipe – "Felipe's Seat" – a chair carved into a rocky outcrop with a great view of the palace, and from where the king is supposed to have watched the building's construction. You can reach it on foot by following the path which starts by the arches beyond the main entrance to the Biblioteca; keep to the left as you go down the hill and then cross the main road and follow the signs. If you have a car, take the M-505 Ávila road and turn off at the sign after about 3km.

▲ LIBRARY IN EL ESCORIAL

Valle de los Caídos

Tues–Sun: April–Sept
10am–6pm; Oct–March
10am–5pm. €5, combined
ticket with El Escorial €8.50
unguided, €10 guided,
free Wed for EU citizens.

Almost at first glance,
this basilica complex,
constructed by Franco
after his Civil War
victory, belies its claim
to be a memorial to
the dead of both sides.

▲ VALLE DE LOS CAÍDOS

The grim, pompous architectural
forms employed, the constant
inscriptions "Fallen for God and
for Spain", and the proximity to
El Escorial clue you in to its true
function – the glorification of
General Franco and his regime.
The dictator himself lies buried
behind the high altar, while the
only other named tomb is that of
his guru, the Falangist leader, José
Antonio Primo de Rivera. The
"other side" is present only in
the fact that the whole thing was
built by the Republican army's
survivors.

From the entrance to the
basilica, a shaky funicular (Tues–
Sun: April–Sept 11am–1.30pm
& 4–6pm; Oct–March 11am–
1.30pm & 3–5.30pm; €2.50)
ascends to the base of a vast cross,
reputedly the largest in the world,
offering superlative views over
the Sierra de Guadarrama and
of the giant, grotesque religious
figures propping up the cross.

Restaurants

Cervecería Los Pescaítos

C/Joaquín Costa 8, El Escorial
☎918 907 720. Daily 1–4pm &
8pm–midnight. A friendly and very
popular local bar serving great
fish dishes and good wine. Tapas
cost €8–10 and a full meal
around €25 a head.

El Charolés

C/Floridablanca 24, El Escorial ☎918
905 975. Daily 1–4pm & 9pm–midnight.
Prestigious and pricey restaurant
renowned for its fish and stews.
They serve a warming *cocido*
in winter on Wednesdays and
Fridays. Around €40 per person.

La Cueva

C/San Antón 4, El Escorial ☎918 901
516, ⊛www.mesonlacueva.com. Tues–
Sun 10.30am–midnight. A good
bet for both tapas and typical
Castilian roasts. Two set menus
at either €16 or €28 (the latter
with *cochinillo*), à la carte will
work out around €35-40.

La Fonda Genara

Plaza de San Lorenzo 2, El Escorial.
☎918 901 636, ⊛www
.restaurantegenara.com. Daily 1.30–4pm
& 9–11.30pm. Low-key but highly
enjoyable place, filled with
theatrical mementos, and offering
a wide range of good quality
Castilian fare. *Menús* available
for around €10–15, otherwise
around €30 per person.

Los Pilares

C/Juan de Toledo 58, El Escorial ☎918
961 972, ⊛www.lospilares.com.
Mon–Sat 1–4pm & 9–11.30pm, Sun
1–4pm. Near the bus station, this
place specializes in re-creating
dishes from the era of Felipe II
– try the capon and bean stew.
Over €30 per person.

Aranjuez and Chinchón

On the edge of the parched plains of New Castille, around fifty kilometres from the capital, is the little oasis town of Aranjuez. Situated at the confluence of the Tajo and Jarama rivers, this is where the eighteenth-century Bourbon rulers set up a spring and autumn retreat. Its opulent palaces and luxuriant gardens inspired composer Joaquín Rodrigo to write the famous Concierto de Aranjuez, while the summer fresas con nata (strawberries with cream), served at roadside stalls, make it a favourite weekend escape for Madrileños.

Nearby is picturesque Chinchón, a small village centred around an atmospheric old plaza lined with traditional mesones (inns) serving quality Castilian food. It's also home to Spain's best-known anís – a mainstay of breakfast drinkers across the country.

The Palacio Real

☎918 910 740, ⓦwww .patrimonionacional.es. Tues–Sun: April–Sept 10am–6.15pm; Oct–March 10am–5.15pm. €4.50 (€5 guided), free Wed for EU citizens. The centrepiece of Aranjuez is the Palacio Real and its gardens (see p.144). Although there has been a royal residence on this site since the late sixteenth century, the present building dates from

---

Visiting Aranjuez and Chinchón

From the end of April to July and September to mid-October, a weekend service on an old wooden steam **train**, the Tren de la Fresa, runs between Madrid and Aranjuez. It leaves Atocha station at 10.05am and departs from Aranjuez at 6pm (information ☎902 228 822). The €26 fare includes a guided bus tour in Aranjuez, entry to the monuments and *fresas con nata* on the train. Standard trains leave every 15–30 minutes from Atocha, with the last train returning from Aranjuez at about 11.30pm.

Buses run every half-hour during the week and every hour at weekends from Estación Sur.

You'll find a helpful **oficina de turismo** in the Casa de Infantes (daily 10am–6.30pm, Oct–May closes 5.30pm; ☎918 910 427, ⓦwww.aranjuez.com & ⓦwww.aranjuez-realsitio.com).

There are hourly buses (#337) from Madrid to Chinchón from the bus station at Avda Mediterraneo 49 near the Plaza Conde Casal, or you can reach the village from Aranjuez on the sporadic service from c/Almíbar 138 (Mon–Fri 4 daily, Sat 2 daily). There's a small **turismo** in the Plaza Mayor (Mon–Fri 10am–8pm, Sat & Sun 11.30am–8pm; ☎918 935 323, ⓦwww.ciudad-chinchon.com).

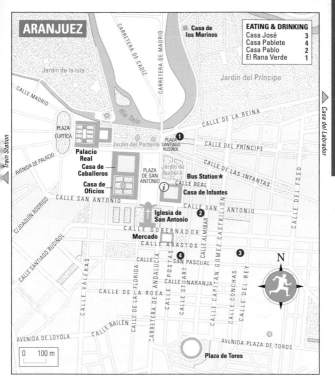

ARANJUEZ

EATING & DRINKING
Casa José	3
Casa Pablete	4
Casa Pablo	2
El Rana Verde	1

Casa de los Marinos

Jardín del Príncipe

Jardín de la Isla

CALLE MADRID

Río Tajo

CARRETERA DE CADIZ

CARRETERA DE MADRID

PLAZA ELÍPTICA

Palacio Real

AVENIDA DE PALACIO

Casa de Caballeros

Casa de Oficios

Jardín del Parterre

PLAZA DE SAN ANTONIO

CALLE SAN ANTONIO

C/JOAQUÍN RODRIGO

PLAZA SANTIAGO RUSIÑOL ❶

Jardín de Isabel II

CALLE DE LA REINA

CALLE DEL PRÍNCIPE

CALLE DE LAS INFANTAS

Bus Station ★

Casa de Infantes

CALLE REAL

CALLE DEL FOSO

CALLE SAN ANTONIO

CALLE CAPITÁN GÓMEZ CASTILLÓN

CALLE ALMIBAR

Iglesia de San Antonio ❷

CALLE GOBERNADOR

Mercado

CALLE ABASTOS

CALLE SANTIAGO RUSIÑOL

CALLE LA FLORIDA

CALLE VALERAS

CALLE DE LA ROSA

CALLE NARANJAL

CALLE POSTAS

CALLE STUART

SAN PASCUAL ❹

❸

CALLE DE ANDALUCÍA

CARRETERA DE ANDALUCÍA

CALLE BAILÉN

AVENIDA DE LOYOLA

CALLE CONCHAS

CALLE DEL REY

AVENIDA PLAZA DE TOROS

Plaza de Toros

N

◁ Train Station

▷ Casa del Labrador

0   100 m

the 1700s and was an attempt by Spain's Bourbon monarchs to create a Spanish Versailles. It isn't in the same league as its French counterpart but is still a pleasant place to while away a few hours, and its three-sided courtyard entrance is impressive enough. The palace is noted more, however, for the ornamental extravaganzas inside than for any virtues of architecture. The seemingly endless number of rooms are all exotically furnished, especially the

Porcelain Room, entirely covered in decorative ware from the factory which once stood in Madrid's Retiro park. The Smoking Room is a copy of one of the finest halls of the Alhambra in Granada, though executed with less subtlety.

▼ ARANJUEZ'S PALACIO REAL

▲ JARDÍN DEL PRINCIPE

Jardín de la Isla and Jardín del Príncipe

Daily: April–Sept 8am–8.30pm; Oct–March 10am–6.30pm. Free. Two palace gardens worthy of a visit are the Jardín de la Isla with its fountains and neatly tended gardens on a small island, and the more attractive Jardín del Príncipe, on the other side of the main road, offering shaded walks along the river and plenty of spots for a siesta.

Casa del Labrador

Jardín del Príncipe. Tues–Sun: June–Sept 10am–6.15pm; Oct–March 10am–5.15pm; visits by appointment only ☎918 910 305. €5, free Wed for EU citizens. At the far end of the Jardín del Príncipe is the Casa del Labrador (Peasant's House), which is anything but what its name implies. The house contains more silk, marble, crystal and gold than would seem possible to cram into so small a place, as well as a huge collection of fancy clocks. Although the hotchpotch of styles will offend purists, this miniature palace still provides a fascinating insight into the tastes of the Bourbon dynasty and the obligatory guided tour

goes into great detail about the weight and value of every item.

Casa de los Marinos

Tues–Sun: April–Sept 10am–6.15pm; Oct–March 10am–5.15pm. €3.40, free Wed for EU citizens. The small Casa de los Marinos, or Museo de Faluas, is a museum containing the brightly coloured launches in which royalty would take to the river. You can do the modern equivalent and take a 45-minute boat trip through the royal parks from the jetty by the bridge next to the palace (summer: Tues–Sun 11am–sunset; €7).

Plaza de Toros

Wed–Sat 10.30am–2pm & 4.30–7.30pm, Sun 10.30am–2pm. Free. Aranjuez's beautiful eighteenth-century Plaza de Toros houses a newly refurbished exhibition space, part of which includes a bullfighting museum with *trajes de luces*, swords and associated memorabilia; the rest traces the town's history and royal heritage. Nearby, look out for c/Naranja and c/Rosa, which contain a number of *corrales*, traditional-style wooden-balconied tenement blocks.

Chinchón

A gentle stroll around the elegant little town of Chinchón, followed by a big lunch at one of its restaurants, is a popular pastime for Madrileños. Noteworthy monuments include a fifteenth-century castle (not open to visitors), a picture-postcard medieval Plaza Mayor, and the Iglesia de la Asunción, with a panel by Goya of *The Assumption of the Virgin*, but it is as the home of **anís** that the town is best known. To sample the local aniseed spirit try one of the local bars or the Alcoholera de Chinchón, a shop on the Plaza Mayor – most visitors come for a tasting before eating at one of the town's traditional *mesones* (see p.146).

If you're visiting over Easter, you'll be treated to Chinchón's own enactment of the Passion

▲ PLAZA MAYOR IN CHINCHÓN

of Christ, though be aware that the town becomes packed with visitors at this time.

In 1995 the town launched its Fiesta del Anís y del Vino, an orgy of *anís* and wine tasting, which, understandably, was an immediate success and is now

CHINCHÓN

EATING & DRINKING
Casa de Pregonero 1
Mesón El Comendador 2
Mesón Cuevas del Vino 3

0   100 m

held mid-April every year. An older annual tradition takes place on July 25, when the feast of St James (*Santiago* in Spanish) is celebrated with a bullfight in the Plaza Mayor.

Restaurants

Casa José

C/Abastos 32, Aranjuez ☎918 911 488. Tues–Sat 1.30–4pm & 8pm–midnight, Sun 1.30–4pm. Closed Aug. Top-class but expensive cuisine at this upmarket restaurant. The house speciality is stuffed artichokes, there is roast goat too, and all the dishes are given a creative twist. Expect to spend at least €50 a head though.

Casa Pablo

C/Almíbar 42, Aranjuez ☎918 911 451. Daily 1–4pm & 8pm–midnight. Closed Aug. A traditional place, the walls of which are covered with pictures of local dignitaries and bullfighters, serving good-value main courses that bring the bill to around €30 per person.

Casa de Pregonero

Plaza Mayor 4, Chinchón ☎918 940 696, ⊛www.lacasadelpregonero. com. Mon & Wed–Sun 1–4pm & 8pm–midnight. Modern touches to traditional dishes, with some great starters and desserts too. The decent-value *menú del día* is €16.80 but à la carte will set you back €35–40 a head.

Mesón El Comendador

Plaza Mayor 21, Chinchón ☎918 940 420. Winter 11am–midnight; summer 11–4pm & 7pm–midnight. Closed Wed. One of the best of a cluster of good restaurants overlooking the beautiful Plaza Mayor, serving classic Castilian fare. Prices around €30–35 a head.

Mesón Cuevas del Vino

C/Benito Hortelano 13, Chinchón ☎918 940 206, ⊛www.cuevasdelvino .com. Mon & Wed–Sat 1.30–4.30pm & 8–11pm, Sun 1.30–4.30pm. Closed Aug. An old olive oil mill which has its own *bodega* (wine cellar) and was a favourite haunt of Orson Welles when he was filming *Chimes at Midnight* here in 1966. You'll need to book at weekends as it's very popular. Excellent roast lamb and *cochinillo* (suckling pig) and some superb starters, all of which will set you back €35–40.

El Rana Verde

Plaza Santiago Rusiñol, Aranjuez ☎918 911 571, ⊛www.aranjuez .com/ranaverde. Daily 8am–midnight. Probably the best-known restaurant in Aranjuez, this pleasant riverside establishment dates back to the late nineteenth century and serves a wide-ranging *menú* at around €13.

Tapas bars

Casa Pablete

C/Stuart 108, Aranjuez. Mon & Wed–Sun 1–4pm & 8pm–midnight. Closed Aug. An offshoot of *Casa Pablo* and one of the best places in town for tapas. Good beer and vermouth too.

Toledo

**Set atop a massive outcrop, every available inch of
which is covered in churches, synagogues, mosques
and houses that cobbled lanes infiltrate as best they
can, Toledo is one of Spain's most fascinating cities.
A former capital, it's surrounded on three sides by the
Río Tajo, and was immortalized by El Greco, who lived
and worked here for most of his later career. The city
itself is a showcase for the many cultures – Visigothic,
Moorish, Jewish and Christian – that have shaped the
destiny of Spain and here left behind a host of sights,
from the Alcázar that looms over the whole town, to
the beautiful cathedral almost hidden in the dense
web of medieval streets. Though Toledo often seems
overrun with visitors, if you have time for just one
day-trip from Madrid, this should be it. Even better, if
you spend the night (see pp.170–171), you'll be able to
enjoy the city's atmosphere without the crowds.**

El Alcázar

C/Carlos V. Closed for refurbishment
until 2008. If one building
dominates Toledo, it's the bluff,
imposing fortress of the Alcázar.
The present building was started
by Carlos V in the sixteenth
century, though it has been
burned and bombarded so often
that almost nothing remaining
is original. The most recent
destruction was in 1936 during
the Civil War, when Nationalist
forces, besieged inside by
the Republican town, were
eventually relieved by an army
heading for Madrid, which then
took severe retribution.

Visiting Toledo

There are **buses** to Toledo from the Estación Sur in Madrid every 30 minutes,
taking about 1hr 15min. The city's bus station is in the modern, lower part of the
city; bus #5 runs from it to central Plaza de Zocódover. A new high-speed train
service from Atocha has cut the journey time to just 35 mins, but the price is up to
€13.76 for a day return ticket and because many of the trains are full you should
purchase in advance (this can be done from most travel agents around the city).
Toledo's train station is about a twenty-minute walk or a bus ride (#5 or #6) from
the heart of town.

   The main **tourist office** (Mon–Sat 9am–7pm, winter Mon–Fri closes 6pm, Sun
& hols 9am–3pm; ☎925 220 843, ⊛www.castillalamancha.es/turismo) is outside
the city walls opposite the Puerta Nueva de Bisagra. There's another office in the
Zococentro shop at c/Sillería 14 in the centre (daily 10.30am–6pm, till 7pm in
summer; ☎925 220 300) and a small information kiosk in the plaza next to the
cathedral (Mon 10.30am–2.30pm, Tues–Sun 10.30am–2.30pm & 4.30–7pm;
☎925 254 030, ⊛www.toledoweb.org).

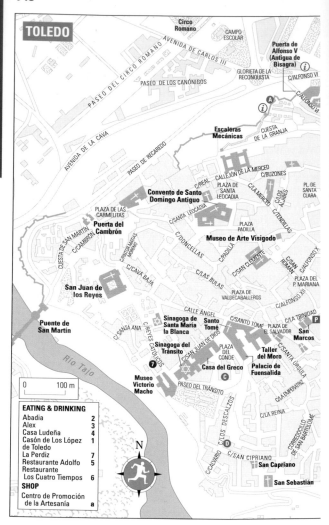

TOLEDO

Circo
Romano

CAMPO
ESCOLAR

Puerta de
Alfonso V
(Antigua de
Bisagra)

AVENIDA DE CARLOS III

PASEO DEL CIRCO ROMANO

GLORIETA DE LA
RECONQUISTA

C/ALFONSO VI

PASEO DE LOS CANÓNIGOS

C/ALFONSO VI

AVENIDA DE LA CAVA

Escaleras
Mecánicas

CUESTA
DE LA GRANJA

PASEO DE RECAREDO

CALLEJÓN DE LA MERCED

C/REAL

PLAZA DE
SANTA
LEOCADIA

C/BUZONES

C/LA MERCED

PL. DE
SANTA
CLARA

Convento de Santo
Domingo Antiguo

C/ALJIBES

C/TENDILLAS

PLAZA DE LAS
CARMELITAS

C/SANTA LEOCADIA

PLAZA
PADILLA

Puerta del
Cambrón

Museo de Arte Visigodo

CUESTA DE SAN MARTÍN

C/CAMBRÓN

C/PINTOR MATÍAS
MORENO

C/DONCELLAS

C/PADILLA

C/SAN CLEMENTE

C/SAN ROMÁN

C/ALFONSO X

C/LAS BULAS

PLAZA DE
P. MARIANA

C/CAVA BAJA

San Juan de
los Reyes

PLAZA DE
VALDECABALLEROS

C/ALFONSO XII

CALLE ÁNGEL

Puente de
San Martín

C/SANTA ANA

C/REYES CATÓLICOS

Sinagoga de
Santa María
la Blanca

Santo
Tomé

C/SANTO TOMÉ

C/LA TRINIDAD

PLAZA DE
EL SALVADOR

San
Marcos

Río Tajo

Sinagoga del
Tránsito

C/SAN JUAN DE DIOS

PLAZA
DEL
CONDE

Taller
del Moro

C/SANTA URSULA

0   100 m

Museo
Victorio
Macho

Casa del Greco

Palacio de
Fuensalida

C/EMPERATRIZ

PASEO DEL TRÁNSITO

C/LA REINA

EATING & DRINKING

Abadía   2
Alex   3
Casa Ludeña   4
Casón de Los López   1
 de Toledo
La Perdiz   7
Restaurante Adolfo   5
Restaurante
 Los Cuatro Tiempos 6

SHOP

Centro de Promoción
 de la Artesanía   a

C/LOS DESCALZOS

CORREDORCILLO
DE SAN BARTOLOMÉ

N

C/CALVARIO

C/SAN CIPRIANO

San Capriano

San Sebastián

After the war, Franco's regime completely rebuilt the Alcázar as a monument to its Civil War defenders.

The interior is in the latter stages of a lengthy refurbishment to convert it into a new Army Museum that will eventually provide a home for all the

exhibits once housed in the Madrid branch.

Hospital y Museo de Santa Cruz

C/Cervantes 3. Mon–Sat 10am–6pm, Sun 10am–2pm. Free during ongoing renovations. A superlative Renaissance building with a

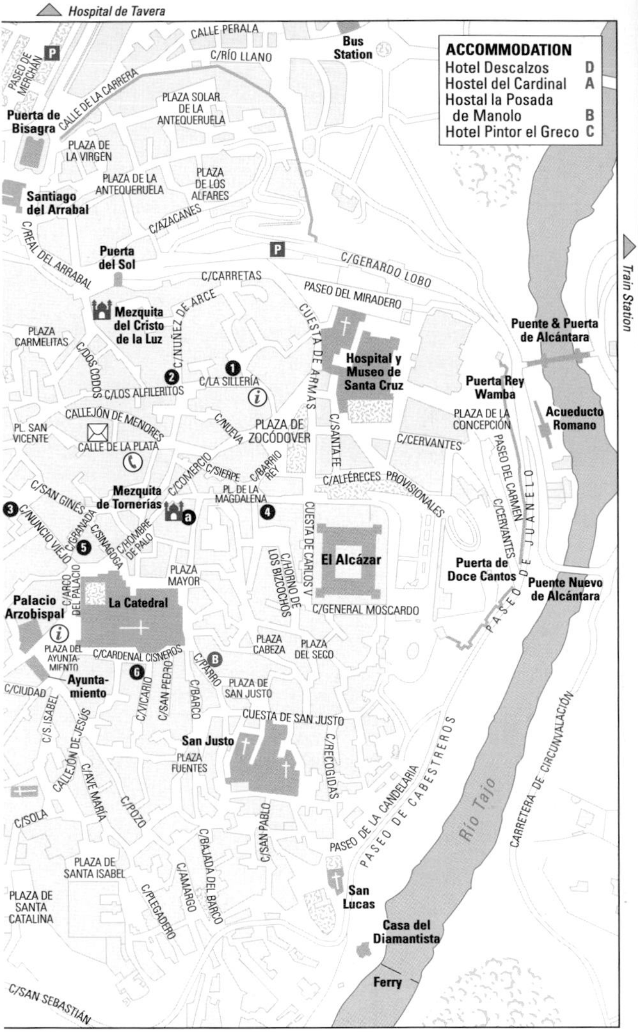
Hospital de Tavera
Train Station
ACCOMMODATION
Hotel Descalzos D
Hostel del Cardinal A
Hostal la Posada de Manolo B
Hotel Pintor el Greco C
CALLE PERALA
C/RÍO LLANO
Bus Station
PASEO DE MERCHÁN
CALLE DE LA CARRERA
Puerta de Bisagra
PLAZA SOLAR DE LA ANTEQUERUELA
PLAZA DE LA VIRGEN
PLAZA DE LA ANTEQUERUELA
PLAZA DE LOS ALFARES
Santiago del Arrabal
C/AZACANES
C/REAL DEL ARRABAL
Puerta del Sol
C/GERARDO LOBO
C/CARRETAS
PASEO DEL MIRADERO
Mezquita del Cristo de la Luz
C/NUÑEZ DE ARCE
PLAZA CARMELITAS
C/DOS CODOS
C/LA SILLERÍA
C/LOS ALFILERITOS
CUESTA DE ARMAS
Hospital y Museo de Santa Cruz
Puente & Puerta de Alcántara
Puerta Rey Wamba
Acueducto Romano
CALLEJÓN DE MENORES
PL. SAN VICENTE
CALLE DE LA PLATA
C/NUEVA
PLAZA DE ZOCÓDOVER
C/SANTA FE
PLAZA DE LA CONCEPCIÓN
C/CERVANTES
PASEO DEL CARMEN
C/COMERCIO
C/SIERPE
C/BARRIO REY
C/ALFÉRECES PROVISIONALES
PASEO DE JUANELO
C/SAN GINÉS
Mezquita de Tornerías
PL. DE LA MAGDALENA
C/NUNCIO VIEJO
C/GRANADA
C/SINAGOGA
C/HOMBRE DE PALO
CUESTA DE CARLOS V
C/HORNO DE LOS BIZCOCHOS
El Alcázar
C/CERVANTES
PLAZA MAYOR
Puerta de Doce Cantos
Puente Nuevo de Alcántara
Palacio Arzobispal
C/ARCO DEL PALACIO
La Catedral
C/GENERAL MOSCARDO
PLAZA DEL AYUNTAMIENTO
C/CARDENAL CISNEROS
PLAZA CABEZA
PLAZA DEL SECO
C/PARRO
Ayuntamiento
C/CIUDAD
C/VICARIO
C/SAN PEDRO
C/BARCO
PLAZA DE SAN JUSTO
C/S.ISABEL
CUESTA DE SAN JUSTO
CALLEJÓN DE JESÚS
San Justo
PLAZA FUENTES
C/RECOGIDAS
PASEO DE CABESTREROS
CARRETERA DE CIRCUNVALACIÓN
C/AVE MARÍA
C/POZO
PASEO DE LA CANDELARIA
Río Tajo
C/SOLA
C/SAN PABLO
C/BAJADA DEL BARCO
PLAZA DE SANTA ISABEL
C/AMARGO
San Lucas
PLAZA DE SANTA CATALINA
C/PLEGADERO
Casa del Diamantista
Ferry
C/SAN SEBASTIÁN

magnificent Plateresque main doorway, this museum houses some of the greatest El Grecos in Toledo, including *The Coronation of the Virgin* and *The Assumption of the Virgin*. As well as outstanding works by Goya and Ribera, there's also a huge collection of ancient carpets and faded tapestries, a military display, sculpture, ceramics and a small archeological collection. The museum is undergoing a long-running renovation programme which entails some temporary reorganization of the exhibits, but remains open to visitors.

▲ TOLEDO'S ALCÁZAR

La Catedral

C/Cardenal Cisneros. Mon–Sat 10.30am–6.30pm, Sun 2–6.30pm. Coro closed Sun am; museums closed Mon. €6, free Wed pm for EU citizens; audio guides €3. Toledo's stunning cathedral reflects the importance of the city that for so long outshone its near neighbour, Madrid. A robust Gothic construction, which took over two hundred and fifty years (1227–1493) to complete, it's richly decorated in almost every conceivable style from these years, with masterpieces of the Gothic, Renaissance and Baroque periods. The cavernous interior is home to some magnificent stained glass, an outstanding *Coro* (Choir), a wonderfully Gothic Capilla Mayor (Main Chapel) and an extravagant high altar. There are also well over twenty chapels embedded in the walls, many containing fine tombs. The cathedral museums are worth a look for their impressive collections including paintings by El Greco, Goya and Velázquez, as well as one of El Greco's few surviving pieces of sculpture.

Convento de Santo Domingo Antiguo

Plaza Santo Domingo Antiguo. Summer: Mon–Sat 11am–1.30pm & 4–7pm, Sun 4–7pm; winter: Sat, Sun & hols only, same hours. €1.80. The Convento de Santo Domingo Antiguo's chief claim to fame is as the resting place of El Greco, whose remains lie in the crypt that can be glimpsed through a peephole in the floor. The convent's religious treasures are displayed in the old choir, but more interesting is the high altarpiece of the church – El Greco's first major commission in Toledo. Unfortunately, most of the canvases have gone to museums and are here replaced by copies.

Santo Tomé and the Burial of the Count of Orgaz

Plaza del Conde ⓦ www.santotome .org. Daily: summer 10am–6.45pm; winter 10am–5.45pm. €1.90, free Wed after 2.30pm for EU citizens. Housed alone, in a small annexe of the church of Santo Tomé, one of the most celebrated attractions of Toledo is El Greco's masterpiece, *The Burial of the Count of Orgaz*. The painting depicts the count's funeral, at

▼ TOLEDO CATHEDRAL

which St Stephen and St Augustine appeared in order to lower him into the tomb. Combining El Greco's genius for the mystic with his great powers as a portrait painter and master of colour, the work includes a depiction of the artist himself – he can be spotted

▲ EL GRECO'S BURIAL OF THE COUNT OF ORGAZ

seventh from the left, looking out at the viewer with his son in the foreground. A search for the count's bones came to an end in early 2001 when they were unearthed from a tomb located, appropriately enough, directly below the painting.

Casa y Museo del Greco

C/Samuel Levi. Closed for refurbishment until 2009. The main paintings which were housed here have been moved to the Museo de Victorio Macho.

Museo de Victorio Macho

Plaza de Victorio Macho ⓦwww .realfundaciontoledo.es. Mon–Sat 10am–7pm, Sun 10am–3pm. €3. Splendidly situated on a spur overlooking the Tajo, this museum contains the sculptures, paintings and sketches of Spanish artist Victorio Macho (1887–1966). The museum is set in a delightfully tranquil garden with the auditorium on the ground floor showing a documentary film (available in English) about the city and its history.

The exhibition space also provides a temporary home to the El Greco paintings, while the Casa y Museo del Greco is being refurbished. Among them is his famous *View and Map of Toledo*, and another full series of the Twelve Apostles, completed later than the set in the cathedral and subtly different in style.

Sinagoga del Tránsito

C/Samuel Levi ⓦwww.museosefardi .net. Tues–Sat 10am–2pm & 4–9pm, Sun 10am–2pm. €2.40. Free Sat pm & Sun. Built along Moorish lines by Samuel Levi in 1366, the Sinagoga del Tránsito became a church after the fifteenth-century expulsion of the Jews and was restored to its original form only in the last century. The interior is a simple galleried hall, brilliantly decorated with polychromed stuccowork and superb filigree windows, while Hebrew inscriptions praising God, King Pedro and Samuel Levi adorn the walls. It also houses a small but engaging Sephardic Museum (same hours) tracing the distinct traditions and development of Jewish culture in Spain.

Sinagoga Santa María la Blanca

C/Reyes Católicos 4. Daily: summer 10am–7pm; winter 10am–6pm. €1.90. Free Wed after 2.30pm with EU passport. The second of Toledo's two surviving synagogues, the fascinating and tranquil Santa

▲ TOLEDO'S JEWISH QUARTER

María la Blanca predates the Sinagoga del Tránsito by over a century. Despite having been both a church and synagogue, the horseshoe arches and the fact that it was built by Mudéjar craftsmen mean it actually looks most like a mosque. The arches are decorated with elaborate plaster designs of pine cones and palm trees, while a fine Baroque *retablo* (altarpiece) dates from the time it was a church. The whole effect is stunning, all set off against a deep-red floor that contains some of the original decorative tiles.

San Juan de los Reyes

C/San Juan de los Reyes 2. Daily: summer 10am–6.45pm; winter 10am–5.45pm. €1.90, free Wed after 2.30pm with passport. The exterior of this beautiful church is bizarrely festooned with the chains worn by the Christian prisoners from Granada released on the reconquest of the city in 1492. It was originally a Franciscan convent founded by the Reyes Católicos (Catholic Monarchs), Fernando and Isabel – who completed the Christian reconquest of Spain – and in which, until the fall of Granada, they had planned to be buried. Its double-storeyed cloister is outstanding, with an elaborate Mudéjar ceiling in the upper floor.

Mezquita del Cristo de la Luz

Cuesta de los Carmelitas Descalzos 10. Daily: summer 10am–2pm & 3.30–7pm; winter 10am–2pm & 3.30–6pm. €1.90, free Wed pm. Although this is one of the oldest Moorish monuments in Spain (the mosque was built by Musa Ibn Ali in the tenth century on the foundations of a Visigothic church), only the nave, with its nine different cupolas, is the original Arab construction. The apse was added when the building was converted into a church, and is claimed to be the first product of the Mudéjar style. The mosque itself, set in a tiny patio-like park and open on all sides to the elements, is so small that it seems more like a miniature summer pavilion, but it has an elegant simplicity of design that few of the town's great monuments can match.

▼ MEZQUITA DEL CRISTO DE LA LUZ

▲ HOSPITAL DE TAVERA

Hospital de Tavera

C/Cardenal Tavera 2. Daily 10am–1pm & 3–5.30pm. €4. A Renaissance palace with beautiful twin patios, the Hospital de Tavera houses the private collection of the Duke of Lerma. The rather gloomy interior is a reconstruction of a sixteenth-century mansion dotted with many fine paintings, while the museum contains several works by El Greco and Ribera's bizarre portrait of a "bearded woman".

Shops

Centro de Promoción de la Artesanía

C/Tornerías. Tues–Sat 10am–2pm & 5–8pm, Sun 10am–2pm. Housed in an old mosque, the Mezquita de las Tornerías, this shop/gallery houses interesting displays of beautiful local crafts, mainly pottery. The renovated eleventh-century building, deconsecrated by the Reyes Católicos around 1500, is worth a visit in itself.

Restaurants

Abadia

Plaza San Nicolás 3. Daily 8am–midnight. Constantly changing menu in this mid-priced restaurant serving specialities such as pheasant *croquetas* and *patatas a lo pobre* (a delicious dish of potatoes fried up with egg, onion and sometimes paprika)

Alex

Plaza de Amador de los Ríos 10, at the top end of c/Nuncio Viejo. Tues–Sun noon–4pm & 8pm–1pm. Reasonable-value restaurant with a much cheaper café attached. *Conejo* (rabbit) and *perdiz* (partridge) are the specialities. Nice location and a shady summer terrace. Around €30 per person.

Casa Ludeña

Plaza Magdalena 13. Daily 1pm–4pm. Closed Wed. One of many places around Plaza Magdalena, this one offers a cheap (around €10) set lunch and the best *carcamusa* (traditional meat stew in a spicy tomato sauce) in town.

Casón de Los López de Toledo

C/Silleria 3. Daily 1.30–4pm & 8.30–11.30pm. Closed Sun eve. Upmarket place in a quiet street, close to Plaza Zocódover. Main courses cost between €15 and €20. Regional specialities and game such as wild boar are on offer.

La Perdiz

C/Reyes Católicos 7. Daily 1–4pm
& 8.30pm–midnight. Quality
restaurant that does a very good
menú de degustación for €21
and has a good selection of
local wines too. Unsurprisingly,
roast partridge (*perdiz*) is the
speciality.

Restaurante Adolfo

C/Granada 6. Daily 1–4pm & 8.30pm–
midnight. ☎925 227 321. Closed
Sun eve & Mon. Tucked behind a
marzipan café, in an old Jewish
town house, this is one of the
best restaurants in town. It
serves very imaginative takes on
traditional Castilian food plus
great desserts, all for around
€45 a head. Be sure to ask to
see the beautiful painted ceiling
downstairs as well.

Restaurante Los Cuatro Tiempos

C/Sixto Ramón Parro 5 ☎925 223
782. Daily 1–4pm & 8.30pm–midnight.
Excellent mid-price restaurant
with local specialities and
good tapas, including delicious
caracoles (snails). The *menú del
día* is around €20 and includes
roast lamb.

Segovia

Strategically sited on a rocky ridge overlooking the Castilian plain, the small city of Segovia contains a panoply of architectural highlights that more than justify a visit. Most celebrated of its many treasures are the Roman aqueduct, the cathedral and the fairy-tale Alcázar, but it's also the less obvious attractions – the ancient churches and mansions from the Golden Age when it was a royal resort and a base for the cortes (parliament) – that add to the city's appeal. Just a few kilometres east stands the Bourbon palace of La Granja, offering an alternative to Segovia's labyrinthine streets, with lavishly furnished rooms and beautifully tranquil gardens.

The Aqueduct

Plaza del Azoguejo. Over 800m long, and at its highest point towering some 30m above the Plaza de Azoguejo, Segovia's aqueduct is an impressive sight. Built without a drop of mortar or cement, it has been here since around the end of the first century AD – no one knows exactly when – though it no longer carries water from the Río Frío to the city. In recent years traffic vibration and pollution have been threatening to undermine the entire structure, but the completion of a meticulous restoration programme should ensure it remains in place for some time to come. For an excellent view

▼ SEGOVIA'S ROMAN AQUEDUCT

Arrival and information

Segovia is an easy day-trip from Madrid, with eight **trains** daily (1hr 50min–2hr) from Atocha and Chamartín stations, as well as up to 31 **buses**, operated by La Sepulvedana and leaving from Paseo de la Florida 11 (Metro Príncipe Pío; 1hr 45min). The city's own train station is some distance out of town – take bus #8 to the central Plaza Mayor; the bus station is on the same route.

There are two **tourist offices** in the **Plaza Mayor**, a local one at no. 6 (daily 9am–8pm; ☎921 466 070, ⓦwww.segoviaturismo.es) and a regional one at no. 10 (Easter & July–Sept daily 9am–9pm; rest of year daily 9am–2pm & 5–8pm; ☎921 460 334, ⓦwww.turismocastillayleon.com). There is a visitor's reception centre in the busy **Plaza de Azoguejo** (daily 10am–8pm; ☎921 466 720) by the aqueduct; all provide maps and information.

A regular bus service from Segovia to La Granja is operated by La Sepulvedana. It leaves from the bus station at Paseo Ezequiel González 12.

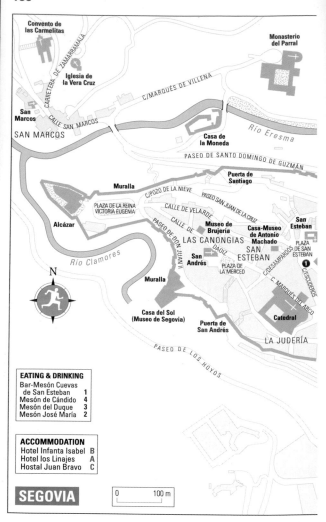

SEGOVIA

0   100 m

of both the aqueduct and the
city, climb the stairs beside it up
to a surviving fragment of the
city walls.

The Cathedral

Plaza Mayor. Mon–Sat: April–Oct
9.30am–6.30pm; Nov–March
9.30am–5.30pm. Sun 9.30am–1.15pm
& 1.30–6.30pm. Free. Museum:
same hours as cathedral, except Sun
opens at 2.30pm. €3. Segovia's
cathedral was the last major
Gothic building constructed in
Spain, and arguably the last in
Europe. Pinnacles and flying
buttresses are tacked on at every
conceivable point, although

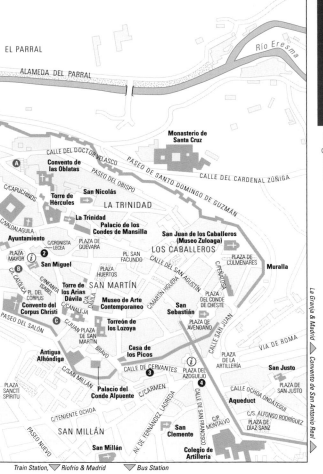

La Granja & Madrid ▷ Convento de San Antonio Real ▷

Train Station, ▽ Riofrio & Madrid   ▽ Bus Station

the interior is surprisingly bare and its space is cramped by a great green marble choir in the very centre. The cathedral's treasures – communion dishes, priestly vestments and so on – are almost all confined to the museum, which is accessed from the cloisters.

The Alcázar

Plaza Reina Victoria Eugenia ⊕www.alcazardesegovia.com. Daily: April–Sept 10am–7pm; Oct–March 10am–6pm. €4, free for EU citizens third Tues in the month. At the edge of town and overlooking the valley of the Río Eresma is the Alcázar, an extraordinary fantasy of a castle.

▲ SEGOVIA'S CATHEDRAL

With its narrow towers and flurry of turrets, it seems eerily familiar to just about every visitor, having served as the model for the original Disneyland castle in California. Although it dates from the fourteenth and fifteenth centuries, it was almost completely destroyed by a fire in 1862 and rebuilt as a deliberately exaggerated version of the original. Inside, the rooms are decked out with armour, weapons and tapestries, but the major attractions are the splendid *artesonado* (wooden sculptured) ceilings and the magnificent panoramas from the tower.

Synagogue-Church of Corpus Cristi

Plaza Corpus Cristi. Mon & Thurs 10am–2pm, Wed & Fri–Sun 10am–2pm & 4–7pm. €1.50. One of the lesser-known sights of Segovia is its synagogue, standing in a little courtyard and now serving as the convent church of Corpus Cristi. It's very similar in style to Santa María la Blanca in Toledo (see p.151), though less refined, and what you see today is actually a reconstruction, as the original was badly damaged by fire during the nineteenth century. Despite all this, it is still of significant historic interest as one of very few surviving synagogue buildings in Spain.

Casa-Museo de Antonio Machado

C/Desamparados 5. Wed–Sun 11am–2pm & 4.30–7.30pm. €1.50, free Wed. This little house displays the spartan accommodation and furnishings of one of Spain's greatest poets of the early twentieth century, Antonio Machado. Though generally associated with the town of Soria, Machado spent the last years of his life teaching here and this museum gives an interesting insight into life during that time.

Museo de Brujería

C/Daoiz. Daily: summer 11am–2pm & 4.30–9pm; winter 11am–2pm

▲ SEGOVIA'S ALCÁZAR

& 4–7pm. €4. The Museum of Witchcraft is of passing interest for most visitors but a compulsory stop for devotees of the dark arts. Some three hundred ghoulish exhibits related to the history of witchcraft and related practices brought together by an Italian collector are on display in this suitably atmospheric house.

Vera Cruz

Carretera Zamarramala. Tues–Sun: summer 10.30am–1.30pm & 3.30–7pm; winter 10.30am–1.30pm & 3.30–6pm; closed Nov. €1.75. This remarkable twelve-sided church stands in the valley facing the Alcázar, and is reached by taking one of the paths that descend from the north side of the city walls. Built by the Knights Templar in the early thirteenth century on the pattern of the Church of the Holy Sepulchre in Jerusalem, it once housed part of the supposed True Cross (hence its name). Today, you can climb the tower for a highly photogenic view of the city, while nearby is a very pleasant riverside walk along the banks of the tranquil Río Eresma.

Convento de San Antonio Real

C/San Antonio Real. Tues–Sat 10am–2pm & 4–7pm, Sun 10am–2pm. €2. If you follow the line of the aqueduct away from the old city for about ten minutes, you will come to a little gem of a palace originally founded by Enrique IV in 1455 and containing an intriguing collection of Mudéjar and Hispano-Flemish art. The convent has some of the most beautiful *artesonado* (wooden sculptured) ceilings in the city and there's a wonderfully detailed fifteenth-century wooden Calvary in the main church.

La Granja

Ⓦ www.patrimonionacional.es. Palace April–Sept Tues–Sun 10am–6pm; Oct–March Tues–Sat 10am–1.30pm & 3–5pm, Sun 10am–2pm. Compulsory guided tour €5, free Wed for EU citizens. Gardens daily: summer 10am–9pm; winter 10am–6pm. €4.50, guided €5, free Wed for EU citizens. The summer palace of La Granja was built by the first Bourbon king of Spain, Felipe V, no doubt in another attempt to alleviate his homesickness for Versailles. Its chief appeal lies in its mountain setting and extravagant wooded grounds and gardens, but it's also worth casting an eye over the palace which, though damaged by a fire in 1918, has been successfully restored. The rooms seen on the tour are furnished in plush French Imperial style and the palace is also home to one of the most valuable collections of sixteenth-century tapestries in the world.

PLACES Segovia

▼ FOUNTAIN AT LA GRANJA

▲ SUCKLING PIG

Outside, the highlight of the eighteenth-century gardens is a series of majestic fountains. They're a fantastic spectacle, with some of the jets rising forty metres, but usually only operate at 5.30pm at weekends and on Wednesdays between Easter and July, with special displays on May 30, July 25 and August 25 (€3.40).

Restaurants

Bar-Mesón Cuevas de San Esteban

C/Valdelaguila 15, off the top end of Plaza San Esteban. Daily noon–midnight. Popular with the locals, this cavern-like restaurant and bar serves up excellent-value tapas and Castilian staples. The *menú del día* is around €10

Mesón de Cándido

Plaza Azoguejo 5 ☎921 428 103. ⊛www.mesondecandido.es. Daily 1.30–4pm & 8–11.30pm. In the shadow of the aqueduct stands the city's most famous restaurant, looked after by the original founder's son and still the place for *cochinillo* (suckling pig) and other roasts. Expect to top €40 if you have the *cochinillo*.

Mesón del Duque

C/Cervantes 12 ☎921 462 487. ⊛www.restauranteduque.es. Daily 1.30–4pm & 8–11.30pm. Rival to the nearby *Cándido*, this place also specializes in Castilian roasts. There are a selection of different *menú* options, but expect to pay over €40 for the works.

Mesón José María

C/Cronista Lecea 11, just off Plaza Mayor ☎921 461 111. Daily 1.30–4pm & 8–11.30pm. The city's best and most interesting restaurant, with modern variations on Castilian classics. The *menú* is a fairly steep €30, but individual dishes cost around €15.

Accommodation

Hotels and hostales

Madrid has plenty of accommodation and most of it is very central. With increasing competition in the sector, many hotels have been busy upgrading facilities in recent years and a new breed of stylish, design-conscious, medium-priced hotel has emerged. The city also has a fair sprinkling of exclusive top-range hotels. If you want a budget place to stay go for one of the *hostales* – small, frequently family-run establishments housed in large, centrally located apartment blocks.

The main factor to consider in choosing a place is location. To be at the heart of the old town, choose the areas around Puerta del Sol, Plaza de Santa Ana or Plaza Mayor; for nightlife, Malasaña or Chueca will appeal; if you want a quieter location and a bit more luxury, consider the Paseo del Prado, Recoletos or Salamanca areas. Another thing to bear in mind is noise. Madrid is a high-decibel city so avoid rooms on lower floors or choose a place away from the action. As for facilities, air conditioning is a welcome extra in summer.

Prices given in our reviews are for the cheapest double room available. Note that hotels add a seven-percent IVA (VAT) charge to the rates given below; for most *hostales* the tax is already included.

Madrid de los Austrias

Hostal La Macarena C/Cava de San Miguel 8, 2º ☎913 659 221, ☎913 642 757, ☎www.silserranos.com. Comfortable family-run *hostal* in a characterful alley near Plaza Mayor. The well-kept rooms are on the small side, but all have bathroom, satellite TV and ceiling fans. It can be a little noisy, but the location is perfect. €65.

Hostal La Perla Asturiana Plaza de Santa Cruz 3 ☎913 664 600, ☎www.perlaasturiana.com. Small, basic rooms in nicely located *hostal* whose higher-class status has now been left a bit behind by modern standards. Doubles have a/c for an extra €5. €52.

Petit Palace Posada del Peine C/Postas 17, ☎915 238 151, ☎www.hthotels.com. This upmarket branch of the *High-tech* hotel

Booking accommodation

Madrid's increasing popularity as a weekend-break destination means that it's best to book accommodation in advance. Phoning or emailing is recommended; most places will understand English. It's also advisable to reconfirm the booking a few days in advance.

Hotels in the more expensive categories run special weekend offers, so it's always worth checking their websites for details. If your Spanish is decent then the bancotel vouchers scheme is a great way of making huge savings on standard rates – they're available online at ☎www.bancotel.es or at travel agents (see p.182).

If you do arrive without a reservation, accommodation services at the airport, the Estación Sur de Autobuses, and Atocha and Chamartín train stations can be useful. Brújula is particularly helpful, with offices at Atocha station (open daily 8.30am–10pm; ☎915 391 173) and Chamartín (daily 7.30am–9pm; ☎913 257 894). The service covers the whole of Spain and there's a €2.50 booking fee.

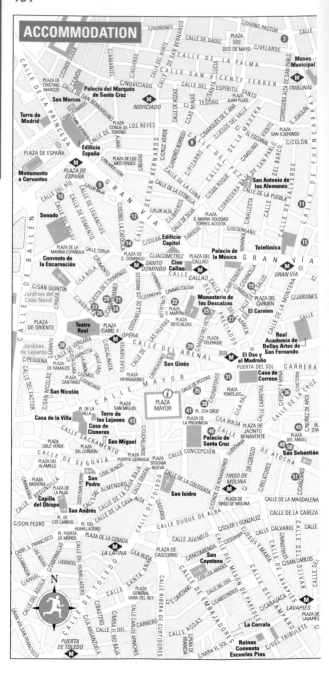

ACCOMMODATION

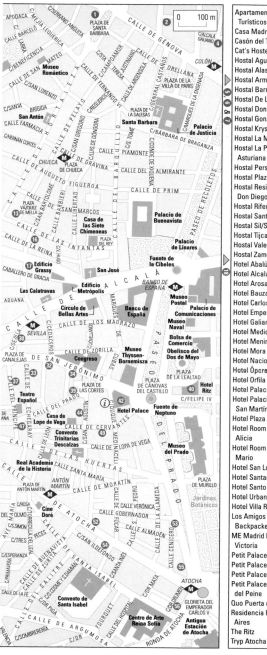

Addresses

Addresses are written in the form "c/Mayor 2, 4°" meaning Mayor street (calle) number two, fourth floor. You may also see *izquierda* (izqda) or *derecha* (dcha), meaning to the left or right of the staircase respectively.

chain is situated in a refurbished building right next to the Plaza Mayor that was once the site of a seventeenth-century inn. Sleek rooms with minimalist decor and stylish fittings. Free Internet access, buffet breakfast. €105–160.

Hotel Plaza Mayor C/Atocha 2 ☎913 600 606, ⊛www.h-plazamayor.com. A stone's throw from the Plaza Mayor and housed in a refurbished historic building, this friendly hotel is perfectly situated and has 31 bright, tastefully decorated, a/c rooms. Excellent value at €80.

Hostal Rifer C/Mayor 5, 4° ☎915 323 197. Spotless, bright rooms, all with en-suite facilities, in the highest – and therefore quietest – of three options in this block. The friendly owner is anxious to please and has plans to upgrade the rooms. €42.

Ópera

Los Amigos Backpackers' Hostel C/Campomanes 6, 4° izda ☎ & ☎915 471 707, ⊛www.losamigoshostel.com. Great backpacking option in a quiet side street, five minutes from Sol. Dormitories cater for 4–6 people, and there are a couple of communal rooms, plus access to the Internet. The friendly staff speak English, and bed linen and use of kitchen are included in the €17–19 price. Doubles available for €45. There is a nearby branch even closer to Sol at c/Arenal 26, 4° ☎915 592 472.

Hotel Carlos V C/Maestro Vitoria 5 ☎915 314 100, ⊛www.hotelcarlosv .com. Large, slightly old-fashioned hotel, behind the Descalzas Reales monastery. Some of the a/c rooms on the fifth floor have balconies (at extra cost), though there isn't much of a view. There's an elegant lounge and café, and the hotel has a deal with a nearby car park which guests can use at reduced rates. €84–125.

Casa Madrid C/Arrieta 2, 2° ☎915 595 791, ⊛www.casademadrid.com. Exclusive boutique-style hotel, offering seven stunning rooms decorated with hand-painted frescoes, classical statues, original paintings and fresh flowers. Ideal for an expensive romantic escape, but not really the place for children. Doubles start at €260, while the suite is €375.

Hostal Don Alfonso Plaza Celenque 1, 2° ☎915 319 840, ☎915 329 225. This clean *hostal* is in a good location close to Sol and has fourteen doubles, two triples and a handful of singles at a competitive price, all with bathrooms and TV. €55.

Hotel Ópera C/Cuesta de Santo Domingo 2 ☎915 412 800, ⊛www .hotelopera.com. This conveniently situated hotel has 79 comfortable rooms, all with free high-speed Internet connection. In keeping with the name, the waiters in the restaurant entertain diners with arias from operas and *zarzuelas*. €120–140.

Hotel Meninas C/Campomanes 7 ☎915 412 805, ⊛www.hotelmeninas.com. A stylish, good-value, 37-room hotel in a quiet street near the Teatro Real. Very helpful staff, excellent attic rooms, flat-screen TVs and free broadband Internet access. Breakfast included. €120.

Hotel Palacio de San Martín C/Plaza de San Martín 5 ☎917 015 000, ⊛www.intur.com/palacio.htm. This former US embassy building is now an elegant hotel offering 94 spacious, classically decorated rooms, a small gym and sauna, plus a fine rooftop restaurant. Price for a double varies but normally somewhere between €150 and €170.

Hotel Room Mate Mario C/Campomanes 4 ☎915 488 548, ⊛www .room-matehotels.com. A hip, designer hotel in a perfect location close to the Teatro Real and next to the trendy *Viuda Blanca* restaurant. Staff are friendly and the ultra-cool rooms, though compact, are well equipped. Buffet breakfast included. Great value with prices from €120. There is a similarly trendy member of the chain, the *Laura*, at Travesía de Trujillos 3 (☎917 011 670) in the plaza by the Descalzas monastery.

Hostal Valencia **Plaza de Oriente 2, 3º ☎915 598 450, ⓦwww.hostalvalencia.tk.** Fabulous location with great views over the plaza towards the Palacio Real. The seven quiet, old-style rooms are very clean and the owner is charming. Highly recommended. €72.

The Rastro, Lavapíes and Embajadores

Hostal Barrera **C/Atocha 96, 2º ☎915 275 381, ⓦwww.hostalbarrera.com.** Upmarket, friendly and good-value 14-room *hostal*, with an English-speaking owner. The a/c rooms are a cut above most found in this category and the bathrooms are modern. One of the best in this part of town. €50.

Cat's Hostel **C/Canizares 6 ☎913 692 807, ⓦwww.catshostel.com.** Certainly not your run-of-the-mill hostel, *Cat's* has a stunning Andalucian patio and subterranean bar. Doubles are available on request, otherwise accommodation is in clean, a/c 4–12-bed dorms. A friendly, fun atmosphere. €19–21.

Tryp Atocha **C/Atocha 83 ☎913 300 500, ⓦwww.trypatocha.solmelia.com.** This large, business-style hotel, which Is not far from Huertas, has 150 modern rooms with all the facilities you'd expect. The usual price for a standard double is around €130, but special offers can bring the price down to €85.

Sol, Santa Ana and Huertas

Hostal Aguilar **Carrera de San Jerónimo 32, 2º ☎914 295 926 or 914 293 661, ⓦwww.hostalaguilar.com.** Large *hostal* offering airy rooms all with bath, TV and a/c. Guests also have access to the Internet. It specializes in multi-bed rooms offering very good prices for quadruples (€84), making it an ideal budget place for families. Doubles are €52.

Hostal Alaska **C/Espoz y Mina 7, 4º dcha ☎915 211 845, ⓦwww.hostalalaska.com.** Four doubles, a triple and a single in this friendly *hostal*, a stone's throw from Sol. All seven of the basic, brightly decorated rooms have bathrooms and TV, and the owner, who speaks English, will go out of his way to make you feel at home. Doubles €50.

Apartamentos Turísticos **C/Príncipe 11 ☎902 113 311, ⓦwww.atprincipe11.com.** A good option for families or groups. The 36 apartments in this centrally located block range from small studios to family suites for up to six, all a/c and with kitchenettes. Prices range from €102 for a four-person to €160 for a family one.

Hostal Armesto **C/San Agustín 6, 1º dcha ☎914 290 940, ⓦwww.hostalarmesto.com.** A standard eight-room *hostal*. All rooms have small bathrooms and TV and the best ones overlook the delightful little garden in the Casa de Lope de Vega next door. Very well positioned for the Huertas/Santa Ana area. €50.

ME Madrid Reina Victoria **Plaza de Santa Ana 14 ☎917 016 000, ⓦwww.memadrid.travel.** Once a favourite haunt of bullfighters, the overblown 192-room *Reina Victoria* has now been refurbished and rebranded as part of Melia's glamorous new *ME* chain of hotels. It comes complete with compulsory minimalist decor, designer furnishings, high-tech fittings, a super cool penthouse bar and a chic restaurant serving fusion-style food. Standard doubles start at around the €200 mark, but special offers can bring the price down to around €170.

Hostal Persal **Plaza del Angel 12 ☎913 694 643, ⓦwww.hostalpersal.com.** Eighty-room *hostal* that is closer to a hotel in terms of services and facilities. The simple, clean rooms all have a/c, bathrooms and TV. There's free Internet access too. Doubles range in price from €65 to €15 depending on the time of year, but It's only worth it if you can get the cheaper rates.

Petit Palace Londres **C/Galdo 2 ☎915 314 105, ⓦwww.hthotels.com.** One of a chain of smart high-tech hotels that offer very good rates and services. This one is in a refurbished mansion and has the trademark swish, well-equipped rooms with a range of facilities. Standard doubles range in price €95–150. There is another member of the chain down the road at c/Arenal 16 (☎915 644 355).

Hostal Plaza D'Ort Plaza del Angel 13, 1º ☎914 299 041, ☻www.plazadort .com. All the smallish rooms in this very clean *hostal* have a shower or bath, TV, telephone and Internet connection, and some have a/c too. Standard doubles cost €48–58.

Quo Puerta del Sol C/Sevilla 4 ☎915 329 049, ☻www.hotelesquo.com. Another of the new generation of style-conscious, mid-range designer hotels. Minimalist decor, swish bathrooms, flat-screen TVs and a great location. Standard rates around €190, but special offers can bring the price down to around €115.

Hotel Room Mate Alicia C/Prado 2 ☎913 896 095, ☻www.room -matehotels.com. Perched on the corner of Plaza Santa Ana, the 34-room *Alicia* is in a great location if a little noisy. Seriously cool decor by interior designer Pascua Ortega, stylish rooms and unbeatable value at €100. There are suites at €120 and €145 with great views over the plaza and if you really want to push the boat out there is a two-floored duplex at €195.

Hotel Santander C/Echegaray 1 ☎914 296 644, ☻www.hotelsantandermadrid .com. Perfectly located for the bars and restaurants in the Santa Ana/Huertas area, this old-fashioned 35-room two-star hotel has spacious and spotless rooms with large bathrooms and classic decor, plus very friendly staff. Good value at €60 for a double.

Hostal Tijcal C/Zaragoza 6, 3º ☎913 655 910, ☻www.hostaltijcal.com. Quirky but extremely friendly *hostal* offering salmon pink rooms (some have good views) with bathroom, TV, very comfortable beds and air conditioning (€5 supplement). Triples and quadruples also available. A sister *hostal*, *Tijcal 2*, is at c/Cruz 26 ☎ 604 628, ☎915 211 477. €54–68 (cheaper if you pay in cash).

Hotel Urban Carrera San Jeronimo 34, ☎917 877 770, ☻www.derbyhotels.es.

An extremely stylish, fashion-conscious, five-star hotel. There are 96 designer rooms, a rooftop pool, a summer terrace and a "pijo" cocktail bar. It even has its own small museum consisting of items from owner Jordi Clos's collection of Egyptian and Chinese art. €230, but look out for special deals on the website.

The Paseo del Arte and the Retiro

Hostal Gonzalo C/Cervantes 34, 3º ☎914 292 714, ☻www .hostalgonzalo.com. One of the most welcoming *hostales* in the city, tucked away close to Paseo del Prado. Twelve bright, ensuite rooms with TV and a fan. The charming owner, Antonio, and his brother Javier run a very smart place at an excellent price. Highly recommended. €50.

Hotel Mediodía Plaza del Emperador Carlos V 8 ☎915 273 060, ☻www .mediodiahotel.com. Huge, slightly faded, good-value 173-room hotel, next to the Reina Sofía and Atocha station. Some of the simple rooms, all of which have bathroom and TV, have been refurbished recently. Directly below, *El Brillante* café does a nice cup of coffee and some decent tapas. €78.

Hotel Mora Paseo del Prado 32 ☎914 201 569, ☻www.hotelmora.com. Friendly, slightly old-fashioned 62-room hotel. All of the refurbished rooms have a/c and some have pleasant views along the Paseo del Prado (double glazing blocks out the worst of the traffic noise). Perfectly positioned for all the galleries and very good value too. €75.

Hotel Nacional Paseo del Prado 48 ☎914 296 629, ☻www.nh-hotels.com. Part of the high-quality *NH* chain, this large, plush hotel is attractively situated opposite the botanic gardens, and is not that pricey, given the excellent facilities and luxurious surroundings. Standard price is €173 but weekend offers bring it down to around €120.

Hotel Palace Plaza de las Cortes 7 ☎913 608 000, ☻www .westinpalacemadrid.com. Colossal, sumptuous hotel with every imaginable facility but none of the snootiness of the *Ritz* across the road. A spectacular, glass-covered central patio and luxurious rooms are part of its charm. Doubles start at around €339, but the price can drop to around €250 with special offers.

The Ritz Plaza de la Lealtad 5 ☎917 016 767, ☯www.ritzmadrid.com. As opulent as you'd expect and popular with celebrities who can obviously bear the pretentious staff. If you want a quick peep, have an early evening cocktail in the leafy garden. The standard rate for a double is a wallet-busting €510, but deals can bring it down to €195.

Hotel Villa Real Plaza de las Cortes 10 ☎914 203 767, ☯www.derbyhotels.es. Classy and very original hotel, complete with its own art collection. Each of the 115 elegant double rooms has a spacious sitting area and the quality rooftop restaurant has fine views towards the Paseo del Prado. Prices start at around €200.

Gran Vía, Chueca and Malasaña

Hotel Arosa C/Salud 21 ☎915 321 600, ☯www.hotelarosa.com. Right in the heart of town, the spacious, a/c rooms in this friendly, well-equipped hotel all have modern bathrooms and a safe. Some of the surrounding streets are a little down-at-heel, but don't let this put you off. Best rate options are €94, but there are occasional cheaper offers too.

Hostal Kryse C/Fuencarral 25, 1º izqda ☎915 311 512, ☯www.breogankryse.com. Welcoming 25-room hostal where all the basic rooms have verandahs, small bathrooms, TV, telephone and ceiling fans. The same people run another hostal in the block. €48.

Hotel De Las Letras Gran Vía 11, ☎915 237 980, ☯www.hoteldelasletras.com. A newly opened, design-conscious hotel housed in an elegant early nineteenth-century building at the smarter end of Gran Vía. Rooms come complete with flat-screen TVs and pillow menus. Downstairs there is a smooth bar and lounge area and a high-quality restaurant with reasonably priced dishes. Standard rate €240, best rate around €150.

Petit Palace Ducal C/Hortaleza 3, ☎915 211 043, ☯www.hthoteles.com. A major upgrade of a former hostal, this is one of a series of self-styled high-tech hotels in which all rooms have high-speed Internet connections and other mod cons. Stylish doubles cost €110.

Hotel San Lorenzo C/Clavel 8, ☎915 213 057, ☯www.hotel-sanlorenzo.com. A former hostal that has been upgraded to a neat and tidy three-star hotel offering clean and comfortable rooms with a/c and bathrooms. Family rooms with two bedrooms are available for between €115-140 €59-90.

Hostal Santa Bárbara Plaza Santa Bárbara 4 ☎914 457 334, ℻914 462 345. Rather upmarket hostal in a good location on a pleasant tree-lined square. The tidy little rooms – some with a/c – all have bathrooms and there's a great Art Deco TV salon too. English spoken. €66.

Hostal Sil/Serrano C/Fuencarral 95, 2º & 3º ☎914 488 972, ☯www.silserranos.com. Two hostales run by a friendly owner at the quieter end of c/Fuencarral. A variety of simple, but comfortable rooms, all with air conditioning, newish bathrooms and TV. From €65.

Hostal Zamora Plaza Vázquez de Mella 1, 4º izqda ☎915 217 031, ☯www.hostalzamora.com. Seventeen simple rooms in an agreeable family-run place, most of which overlook the plaza. Some rooms have a/c, and all have modern bathrooms and TV. If you can't get in here, there are three other similar hostales in the same block. €45–50.

Salamanca

Hotel Alcalá C/Alcalá 66 ☎914 351 060, ☯www.nh-hotels.com. Large, classy hotel belonging to the efficient NH chain, just to the north of the Retiro, with smart rooms, professional staff, laundry facilities and a car park. Expensive, but good deals available during the summer and at weekends. Standard price is around €165, but special weekend offers can bring it down as low as €75.

Hotel Bauza C/Goya 79 ☎914 357 545, ☯www.hotelbauza.com. A sophisticated feel to this modern hotel close to the Salamanca shops and Plaza Colón. Tasteful, well-equipped rooms and good service. Prices start from around €160, but Internet offers can bring the price down to around €130.

Hostal Residencia Don Diego C/Velázquez 45, 5° ☎914 350 760, ⓦwww.hostaldondiego.com. Comfortable, friendly, medium-sized *hostal* in an upmarket area of town. The quiet rooms, with full facilities, newly equipped bathrooms, a/c and satellite TV, are reasonably priced for the area. Some English-speaking staff. €96.

Hotel Galiano C/Alcalá Galiano 6 ☎913 192 000, ⓦwww.hotelgaliano .com. Hidden away in a quiet street, this small hotel has a sophisticated air about it. There's a pleasant, well-furnished salon off the entrance lobby, staff are polite and the classic-style rooms are a/c. Breakfast costs €6. Car parking available. €120.

Hotel Orfila C/Orfila 6 ☎917 027 770, ⓦwww.hotelorfila.com. An exclusive boutique hotel housed in a beautiful nineteenth-century mansion in a quiet street north of Alonso Martínez. Twelve of the exquisite rooms are suites, there is an elegant terrace for tea and drinks and an upmarket restaurant, too. Of course none of this comes cheap, with rooms starting at €380 a night.

Hotel Petit Palace Embassy C/Serrano 46 ☎914 313 060, ⓦwww.hthotels .com. A newly opened member of the sleek *High-tech* chain of hotels. This one, which is close to Plaza Colón and in the middle of the upmarket Salamanca shopping district, has 75 rooms, including 10 family ones for up to four people. Free broadband Internet access and flat-screen TVs. From €150.

Plaza de España

Hotel Abalú C/Pez 19, 1° ☎915 314 744, ⓦwww.hotelabalu.com. Another of the new arrivals on the Madrid hotel scene. This one, which Is just north of Gran Vía, has just 10 Luis Delgado-designed rooms,

each one brimming with individual touches such as mini-chandeliers, butterfly prints and patterned mirrors. Personal service guaranteed and great value, too, with doubles starting at just €87.

Residencia Buenos Aires Gran Vía 61, 2° ☎915 420 102 or 915 422 250, ⓦwww.hoteleshn.com. A former *hostal* recently upgraded to a thirty-room hotel, whose pleasantly decorated rooms have a/c, satellite TV and modern bathrooms, plus double glazing to keep out much of the noise. €60.

Casón del Tormes C/Río 7 ☎915 419 746, ⓦwww.hotelcasondeltormes.com. Welcoming three-star place in a surprisingly quiet street next to Plaza de España. The 63 a/c, en-suite rooms are very comfortable and hotel facilities include a bar and breakfast room, and helpful, English-speaking staff. €69 in July & Aug, €102 otherwise.

Hotel Emperador Gran Vía 53 ☎915 472 800, ⓦwww.emperadorhotel.com. The only real reason to come here is the superb rooftop swimming pool with its magnificent views, while the hotel itself is geared up for the organized tour market and is rather impersonal. The rooms are large and well decorated though. €112–122.

Hotel Santo Domingo Plaza Santo Domingo ☎915 479 800, ⓦwww .hotelsantodomingo.net. Modern, attractively decorated rooms in this well-run and friendly hotel. Some of the more expensive ones have small terraces; all have a/c, satellite TV, minibars and a safe. €114–123.

Toledo

See map, p.148.

Hostal Cardenal Paseo de Recaredo 24 ☎925 224 900, ⓦwww .hostaldelcardenal.com. A splendid old palace with a renowned restaurant and delightful gardens, located outside the city wall, near Puerta de Bisagra and the electric staircase up to the old part of town. €112.

Hostal Descalzos C/Descalzos 30

☏925 222 888, ⊛www.hostaldescalzos
.com. Very good-value, centrally
located *hostal*, handy for the main sights.
Some of the a/c en-suite rooms have nice
views, plus there's a small open-air pool.
€50-60.

**Hotel Pintor el Greco C/Alamillos de
Transito 13** ☏925 285 191, ⊛www
.hotelpintorelgreco.com. Well-equipped
and nicely furnished hotel in a refurbished
seventeenth-century bakery in the old Jewish quarter. Many of the 33 rooms have fine
views across the Rió Tajo. €110–124.

**Hostal La Posada de Manolo
C/Sixto Ramón Parro 8** ☏925 282 250,
⊛www.laposadademanolo.com. An
atmospheric, fourteen-room *hostal* in a
carefully refurbished period house close to
the cathedral. €72.

Segovia

See map, p.156.

Hotel Infanta Isabel Plaza Mayor 12
☏921 461 300, ⊛www
.hotelinfantaisabel.com. Comfortable new
hotel with 39 spacious, a/c rooms, housed
in a renovated nineteenth-century building
right on the Plaza Mayor. €97.

Hostal Juan Bravo C/Juan Bravo 12
☏921 463 413. This good, budget option
has comfy rooms and plant-festooned
bathrooms. €40.

Hotel Los Linajes C/Dr Velasco 9
☏921 460 475, ⊛www.loslinajes.com.
Good-value cosy hotel, set in part of an
old palace. It has a fine garden overlooking
the river valley, and all rooms are a/c. Own
parking too. €99.

Essentials

Arrival

Whatever your point of arrival, it's easy to get into the centre of Madrid. The airport is connected by metro, shuttle buses and taxis, while the city's main train and bus stations are linked to the metro system.

By air

The **Aeropuerto de Barajas** (information ☎ 902 404 704, ⓦ www.aena.es) is 16km east of the city. It has four terminals, including the vast new T4 building designed by Richard Rogers and Carlos Lamela, which has helped double capacity to some 70 million passengers a year. All Iberia's domestic and international flights, as well as airlines that belong to the Oneworld group, such as British Airways, Aer Lingus and American Airways, use T4 (a 10min shuttle bus ride from the other terminals); most other international flights including Easyjet, go from T1.

From the airport, the **metro link** (Line 8) takes you from T4 and T2 to the city's Nuevos Ministerios station in just fifteen minutes (daily 6am–2am; €2. Check-in facilities for a handful of airlines are available here for your return journey). From there, connecting metro lines take you to city-centre locations in about fifteen minutes.

The route by road to central Madrid is more variable, depending on rush-hour traffic, and can take anything from twenty minutes to an hour. Buses run from each terminal to Avenida América (#200 from T1 and T2, #204 from T4; daily 6am–11.30pm; €1.75). Taxis are always available outside, too, and cost around €25 to the centre, unless you get stuck in traffic.

By land

Trains from France and northern Spain arrive at the **Estación de Chamartín**, a modern terminal in the far north of the city, connected by metro with the centre, and by regular commuter trains (*trenes de cercanías*) to the much more central **Estación de Atocha**. Atocha has two interconnected terminals: one for local services; the other for all points in southern and eastern Spain, including the high-speed AVE services to Sevilla, Zaragoza and Barcelona. For train information **and reservations** call ☎ 902 240 202 or go to ⓦ www.renfe.es.

Bus terminals are scattered throughout the city, but the largest – used by all of the international bus services – is the **Estación Sur de Autobuses** at c/Méndez Álvaro 83, 1.5km south of Atocha train station (☎ 914 684 200, ⓦ www.estaciondeautobuses.com; Metro Méndez Álvaro).

Arriving **by car**, all main roads into Madrid bring you right into the city centre, although eccentric signposting and even more eccentric driving can be unnerving. The inner ring road, the M-30, and the Paseo de la Castellana, the main north–south artery, are both notorious bottlenecks, although virtually the whole city centre can be close to gridlock during **rush-hour periods** (Mon–Fri 7.30–9.30am & 6–8.30pm). Be prepared for a long trawl around the streets to find **parking** and even when you find somewhere, in most central areas you'll have to buy a ticket at one of the roadside metres (€2.55 for a maximum stay of two hours in the blue-coloured bays; €1.80 for a maximum stay of one hour in the green-coloured bays. Charges apply Mon–Fri 9am–8pm, Sat and Aug 9am–3pm). Another option is to put your car in one of the many signposted *parkings* (up to €1.80 for an hour and around €15 for a day). Once in the city, and with public transport being both efficient and good value, your own vehicle is really only of use for out-of-town excursions.

Information

There are year-round **turismo offices** at several points across the city (see below for details), supplemented by **booths** near the Prado, Cibeles, the Palacio Real and in Plaza del Callao off Gran Vía which can provide information about all the major sights and tourist services. The Madrid tourist board's website (🌐 www.esmadrid.com) has details on accommodation and eating out, as well as tours and events; the regional authority's site (🌐 www.turismomadrid .es) has similar information covering the whole of the Madrid province. You can **phone for tourist information** in English on ☏ 902 100 007, a premium rate number that links all the regional turismo offices mentioned below, and on ☏ 901 300 600 and ☏ 010 (or ☏ 915 404 040 if you are phoning from outside Madrid).

Listings information is in plentiful supply in Madrid. The **newspapers** *El País* (🌐 www.elpais.es) and *El Mundo* (🌐 www.metropoli.es) have excellent daily listings (in Spanish), and on Friday both publish sections devoted to events, bars and restaurants in the capital. If your time in Madrid doesn't coincide with the Friday supplements, or you want a full rundown, pick up the weekly **listings**

magazine *La Guía del Ocio* (🌐 www .guiadelocio.com; €1) at any newsagent's stand. The ayuntamiento (city council) also publishes a monthly what's-on pamphlet, *En Madrid* (in English and Spanish), free from any of the tourist offices. Finally, *In Madrid* (🌐 www.in-madrid.com) is a free monthly magazine, available in bars, that features useful reviews of nightlife.

For getting around, the **maps** in this book should be enough for navigating the centre, or there's the *Rough Guide City Map Madrid* that pinpoints sights, hotels, restaurants and bars. Free maps of the city are also available from any of the turismos.

Tourist offices

Barajas International Airport T1 & T4 T1: Mon–Sat 8am–8pm, Sun 9am–2pm ☏ 913 058 656. T4: daily 9.30am– 8.30pm; ☏ 913 338 248.
Estación de Atocha Mon–Fri 9am–8pm, Sat & Sun 9am–1pm; ☏ 902 100 007. Metro Atocha Renfe.
Estación de Chamartín Mon–Fri 8am– 8pm, Sat 9am–2pm; ☏ 913 159 976. Metro Chamartín.
Plaza Mayor 27 Daily 9.30am-8.30pm ☏ 915 881 636. Metro Sol.
C/Duque de Medinaceli 2 Mon–Fri 9am–7pm, Sat 9am–3pm ☏ 914 294 951. Metro Banco de España.

The Madrid card

The Madrid tourist card (☏ 902 877 996, 🌐 www.madridcard.com and 🌐 www .neotourism.com) gives the holder use of public transport, admission to 40 major museums, a tour of the Bernabéu, the teleférico, an open-top bus tour and a guided walk of the old city, plus discounts at a number of shops and restaurants. It costs €39 for one day (€49 for two, €59 for three) and is on sale at the Plaza Mayor, Atocha Station and c/Duque de Medinaceli tourist offices. There is a variation known as the Madrid Card Cultura directed solely at the museums (from €25 a day) and a children's version for under-12s (€29 for 72 hours). Do your sums before you splash out though, as you need to cram a lot into a day's sightseeing to get your money's worth and if you want to concentrate on the big three art galleries, the Paseo del Arte ticket (see p.90) is far better value and allows you to take things at a more leisurely pace.

City transport

Madrid is an easy city to get around. The central areas are walkable, the metro is modern and efficient, buses serve out-of-the-way districts, and taxis are always available.

If you're using public transport extensively it's worth thinking about getting a **tourist pass** (*abono túristico*) covering the metro, train and bus. These are non-transferable and you'll need to show your passport or identity card at the time of purchase. Zone A cards cover central Madrid, Zone T cards cover the whole region including Toledo and Guadalajara but not the airport buses. They are available for a duration of one to seven days and range in cost from €3.80 for a Zone A daily card to €39.60 for a weekly one for Zone T (under-11s are half price, under-4s are free). If you are staying longer, passes (*abonos*) are available for a calendar month. They are available at *estancos* (tobacconists and stamp shops identified by a yellow and brown sign) and metro stations.

The metro

The clean and efficient **metro** (🅦 www .metromadrid.es) is by far the quickest way of getting around Madrid, serving most places you're likely to want to get to. It runs from 6am until 2am and the flat fare is €1 for the central zone stations (€1.75 if you want to venture into the outer zone), or €6.40 for a ten-trip ticket (*bono de diez viajes*) in either the central or outer zone, which can be used on buses too. The network has undergone massive expansion in recent years and some of the outlying commuter districts are now connected by light railways which link with the existing metro stations. Lines are numbered and colour-coded, and the direction of travel is indicated by the name of the terminus station. You can pick up a free colour map of the system (*plano del metro*) at any station.

Buses

The comprehensive **bus network** (🅦 www.emtmadrid.es) is a good way to get around and see the sights. There are information booths at Plaza de Cibeles and Puerta del Sol, which dispense a huge route map (*plano de los transportes de Madrid*) and also sell bus passes. Fares are the same as the metro, at €1 a journey, or €6.40 for a ten-trip ticket (*bono de diez viajes*) which can be used on both forms of transport. When you get on the bus, punch your ticket in a machine by the driver. You can also buy tickets from the driver, but try and have the right money.

Useful bus routes

#2 From west to east: from Argüelles metro station running along c/Princesa, past Plaza de España, along Gran Vía, past Cibeles and out past the Retiro.

#3 From south to north: Puerta de Toledo, through Sol, up towards Gran Vía and then Alonso Martínez and northwards.

#5 From Sol via Cibeles, Colón and the Paseo de la Castellana to Chamartín.

#27 From Embajadores, via Atocha, up the length of the Castellana to Plaza de Castilla.

#33 From Príncipe Pío out via the Puente de Segovia to the Parque de Atracciones and Zoo in Casa de Campo.

#C The Circular bus route takes a broad circuit round the city from Atocha, via Puerta de Toledo, Plaza de España, Moncloa, Cuatro Caminos, Avenida de América and Goya.

Services run from 6am to midnight, with *búho* (owl) buses operating through the night on twenty routes around the central area and out to the suburbs: departures are half-hourly midnight–5.30am from Plaza de Cibeles and Puerta del Sol.

Taxis

Madrid has thousands of reasonably priced **taxis** that you can wave down on the street – look for white cars with a diagonal red stripe on the side. Seven euro will get you to most places within the centre and, although it's common to round up the fare, you're not expected to tip. The minimum fare is €1.85 (€2.90 at weekends) and supplements (€2.50–€5) are charged for baggage, going to the airport, train and bus stations or outside the city limits, and for night trips (11pm–7am). To phone for a taxi, call ☎915 478 600 (also for wheelchair-friendly cabs), ☎914 051 213, ☎913 712 131 or ☎914 473 232. If you want to make a complaint, take the driver's number and ask for the *hoja de reclamaciones* (a claim form). If you leave something in a taxi ring ☎915 884 348.

Local trains

The **local train** network, or Cercanías, is the most efficient way of connecting

---

City tours

The turismo in Plaza Mayor (see p.49) can supply details of guided English-language **walking tours** around the city on the "Descubre Madrid" programme; these cost from €3.25 (10am most mornings from the Plaza Mayor tourist office; info at ⓦwww.esmadrid.com and ☎915 882 906 & 915 881 636). For a **bus tour** of all the major sights try Madrid Vision at c/Felipe IV between the Prado and the *Ritz* hotel (☎917 651 016, ⓦwww.madridvision.es); tickets cost €15.40 (children €8.30, under-7s free) and allow you to jump on and off at various points throughout the city. Pick-up points include Puerta del Sol, Plaza de España and the Prado.

---

between the main railway stations and also provides the best route out to many of the suburbs and nearby towns. Most trains are air-conditioned, fares are cheap and there are good connections with the metro. Services generally run every fifteen to thirty minutes from 6am to midnight. For more information go to the RENFE website at ⓦwww.renfe.es and click on the Cercanías section for Madrid.

Festivals and events

In common with the rest of Spain, Madrid is not short of **festivals**, some involving the whole city, others just an individual barrio. The more important dates celebrated in the capital are listed below.

Also worth checking out are **cultural events** organized by the city council, in particular the Veranos de la Villa (July–Sept) and Festival de Otoño (Sept–Nov) which include concerts (classical, rock, flamenco), theatre and cinema. Many events are free and, in the summer,

often open air, taking place in the city's parks and squares. Annual festivals for alternative theatre (Feb), flamenco (Feb), books (end of May), dance (April–May), photography (mid-June to mid-July) and jazz (Nov) are also firmly established on the cultural agenda. Information on all events can be found in the listings sources on p.176 and on the city's website ⓦwww.esmadrid.com.

Museums usually close on Jan 1, Jan 6, May 1, Dec 24, 25 and 31.

January

Cabalgata de los Reyes (Cavalcade of the Three Kings) To celebrate the arrival of the gift-bearing Three Kings, the evening of January 5 sees a procession through the centre of Madrid in which children are showered with sweets. It's held on the evening before presents are traditionally exchanged in Spain.

February–April

Carnaval Held the week before Lent, this is the excuse for a lot of partying and fancy-dress parades, especially in the gay zone around Chueca. The end of *Carnaval* is marked by the bizarre and entertaining parade, *El Entierro de la Sardina* (The Burial of the Sardine), on the Paseo de la Florida. **Semana Santa** Easter week is celebrated with a series of solemn processions around Madrid, with Jueves Santo (Maundy Thursday) and Viernes Santo (Good Friday) both public holidays in the city. Toledo also has very popular parades against the impressive backdrop of the city's ancient streets (routes and times of processions are available from tourist offices).

May

Fiesta del Dos de Mayo The May 2 celebrations around Madrid, but particularly in Malasaña, are held to commemorate the city's uprising against the French in 1808. Bands and partying take place around the main festive focus, Plaza Dos de Mayo. **Fiestas de San Isidro** Madrid's patron saint's day, May 15, is marked with festivities – some of the biggest in the country – that actually spread over a week. The non-stop round of carnival events includes parades and loads of free entertainment, and usually centres on Plaza Mayor. Evenings generally start out with traditional *chotis* music and dancing, and there are also bands playing each night

in the Jardines de las Vistillas (south of the Palacio Real). The fiestas also herald the start of the bullfighting season. **La Feria del Libro** At the end of May, Madrid's great book fair takes place with hundreds of stands set up in the Retiro Park.

June–July

Gay Pride Week Usually celebrated at the end of June or beginning of July, Gay Pride is a week-long party throughout Chueca culminating in a massive carnival-style parade that brings the city centre to a standstill.

August

Castizo fiestas From August 6 to 15, authentic Madrileños put on lively, traditional fiestas to celebrate the saints' days of *San Cayetano, San Lorenzo* and *La Virgen de la Paloma*. Taking place across the areas of La Latina and Lavapiés, much of the activity centres around Calle Toledo, the Plaza de la Paja and the Jardines de las Vistillas.

December

Navidad The Christmas period in Madrid sees Plaza Mayor taken over by a model of a nativity crib and a large seasonal market with stalls selling all manner of festive decorations. El Corto Inglés department store, at the bottom of c/Preciados, has an all-singing-all-dancing clockwork Christmas scene that plays at regular intervals during the day to the delight of assembled children. **Noche Vieja** New Year's Eve is celebrated at bars, restaurants and parties all over the city, and there are bands in some of the squares. Puerta del Sol is the customary place to gather for midnight, waiting for the strokes of the clock and then attempting to swallow a grape on each strike to bring good luck in the coming year.

Directory

Addresses Calle (street) is abbreviated to c/ in addresses, followed by the number on the street, then another number that indicates the floor, eg c/Gijón 23, 5° means fifth floor of no. 23 Gijón Street. You may also see *izquierda* and *derecha*, meaning left or right (apartment or office) of the staircase.

Airlines Aer Lingus ☎902 502 737, ⓦwww.aerlingus.com; Air Europa ☎902 401 501, ⓦwww.aireuropa.com; Air France ☎901 112 266, ⓦwww.airfrance.com; Alitalia ☎902 100 323, ⓦwww.alitalia.com; American Airlines ☎902 115 570, 912 702 536, ⓦwww.aa.com; British Airways ☎902 111 333, 913 874 365, ⓦwww.ba.com; Brussels Airlines ☎807 220 003, ⓦwww .brusselsairlines.com; EasyJet ☎902 299 992, ⓦwww.easyjet.com; Iberia ☎902 400 500, ⓦwww.iberia.com; KLM ☎902 222 747, ⓦwww.klm.com; Lufthansa ☎902 220 103, ⓦwww.lufthansa.com; Ryanair ☎807 220 032, ⓦwww.ryanair.com.

Banks and exchange Banks are plentiful throughout the city and are the best places to change money. Opening hours are normally Mon–Fri 9am–2pm, but some banks also open Sat 9am–1pm from October to May. Branches of El Corte Inglés have exchange offices with long hours and reasonably competitive rates; the most central is on c/Preciados, close to Puerta del Sol. Barajas Airport also has a 24-hour currency exchange office. The rates at the exchange bureaux scattered around the city are often very poor, though they don't usually charge commission.

ATM **cash machines** (cajeros automáticos) are widespread and accept most credit and debit cards. They're often the most convenient way to get cash, though it's wise to have a back-up source of funds. Credit cards are widely accepted in hotels, restaurants and shops.

Car rental Major operators have branches at the airport and train stations. Central offices include: Atesa Atocha ☎902 100 101, 915 061 846, ⓦwww.atesa.com; Avis Gran Vía 60 ☎915 484 204, reservations ☎902 180 854, ⓦwww.avisworld.com; Europcar c/San Leonardo 8 ☎915 418 892, ⓦwww .europcar.com; Hertz Atocha Station ☎914 681 318, reservations ☎913 729 300 ⓦwww.hertz.com. Easy-Rent-a-Car Chamartín at c/Agustín de Foxa 29, Ronda de Atocha 10, Gran Vía 80 ☎902 360 535 (telephone bookings available from Britain only), ⓦwww.easycar.com; Pepecar at Atocha and Chamartín stations ☎807 414 243 ⓦwww.pepecar.com.

Children Many of Madrid's main sights lack children-specific activities, but there's plenty to keep kids occupied during a short stay, from various parks – the Retiro being a particular favourite (see p.98) – to swimming pools (see p.182), the attraction park (see p.135) and the zoo (see p.134). There is also a well-set-up ecological theme park/zoo

on the outskirts of the city (ⓦwww .faunia.es). Children are, in general, doted on in Spain and welcome in nearly all cafés and restaurants.

Cinema Madrileños love going to the cinema (cine) and, though most foreign films are dubbed into Spanish, a number of cinemas have original-language screenings, listed in a separate versión original/subtitulada (v.o.) section in the newspapers. Tickets cost €6–7 but most cinemas have a día del espectador (usually Mon or Wed) with a reduced admission charge. Be warned that on Sun night what seems like half of Madrid goes to the movies and queues can be long. The most central cinemas showing v.o. films include the two Renoirs on c/Martín de los Heros and c/Princesa, and the Princesa on c/Princesa 3, all next to Plaza de España, and the nine-screen Ideal Yelmo Complex, c/Doctor Cortezo 6, south off c/Atocha and near Plaza Santa Ana.

Disabilities, Travellers with Madrid is not particularly well geared up for disabled visitors (minusválidos), although the situation is gradually improving. The Organización Nacional de Ciegos de España (ONCE; National Organisation for the Blind, c/Prim 3 ☎915 325 000, ⓦwww.once .es) provides specialist advice, as does the Federación de Asociaciones de Minusválidos Físicos de la Comunidad de Madrid (FAMMA, c/Galileo 69 ☎915 933 550, ⓦwww.famma.org). The website ⓦwww .discapnet.es is a useful source of information (Spanish only). Wheelchair-accessible taxis can be ordered from Radio Taxi (☎915 478 200 or 915 478 600).

Embassies Australia Plaza Descubridor Diego Ordás 3 ☎913 536 600, ⓦwww .embaustralia.es; Britain c/Fernando el Santo 16 ☎913 190 200, ⓦwww.ukinspain.com (British Consulate; Paseo de Recoletos 7–9 ☎915 249 700); Canada c/Núñez de Balboa 35 ☎914 233 250, ⓦwww.canada-es.org; Ireland Paseo de la Castellana 46 ☎914 364 093; New Zealand Plaza Lealtad 2 ☎915 230 226, ⓦwww.nzembassy.com /home.cfm?c=27; USA c/Serrano 75 ☎915 872 200, ⓦwww.embusa.es; South Africa c/Claudio Coello 91 ☎914 363 780.

Emergencies For police, medical services and the fire brigade call ☎112.

Entrance fees Madrid's clutch of top-notch museums, galleries and palaces often offer free entrance on certain days of the week. Sites classed as Patrimonio Nacional such as the Palacio Real, the Convento de la Encarnación, El Pardo and the Monasterio de las Descalzas are free to EU citizens on Wed (bring your passport). Many museums run by Madrid City Council including the Museo Municipal, the Museo de San Isidro, La Ermita de San Antonio and the Templo de Debod no longer charge admission at all. Most museums are free for under-18s and give substantial discounts to retired visitors and students (bring ID in all cases). In addition, many places that normally charge entry set aside certain times when entrance is free (see our reviews for details) and nearly all of them throw their doors open on May 18, International Museum Day.

Gay and lesbian visitors The main gay organization in Madrid is Coordinadora Gay de Madrid, c/Puebla 9 (Mon–Fri 10am–2pm & 5–8pm; ☎915 224 517, ✆www.cogam.org), which can give information on health, leisure and gay rights, and produces its own free monthly newsletter. Feminist and lesbian groups are based at the Centro de la Mujer, c/Barquillo 44, 1° izda ☎913 193 689. For a good one-stop shop with lots of info on the gay scene, try Berkana Bookshop, c/Hortaleza 64 (Mon–Sat 10.30am–9pm; Sun noon–2pm & 5–9pm; ✆www.libreriaberkana.com).

Hospitals El Clínico San Carlos c/Profesor Martín Lagos s/n ☎913 303 000; Hospital Gregorio Marañon c/Dr Esquerdo 46 ☎915 868 000; Ciudad Sanitaria La Paz Paseo de la Castellana 261 ☎917 277 000. First-aid stations are scattered throughout the city and open 24 hours: one of the most central is at c/Navas de Tolosa 10, just south of Plaza Callao (☎915 210 025). English-speaking doctors are available at the Anglo-American Medical Unit, c/Conde de Aranda 1 ☎914 351 823; Mon–Fri 9am–8pm, Sat 10am–3pm.

Internet access Workcenter on Plaza Canalejas (daily 8am–11pm, ☎913 601 395, Metro Sevilla), Vortex, c/Ave María 20 (daily 10am–midnight, Metro Lavapiés), Café Comercial on the Glorieta de Bilbao (upstairs, Metro Bilbao) and La Casa de Internet at c/Luchana 20 (Metro Bilbao) are well-equipped, central Internet cafés. Prices range from €1 to €3.50 an hour.

Left luggage There are left-luggage facilties (consignas) at Barajas Airport in terminals 1, 2 and 4 (open 24 hours; €3.60 for up to 24 hours and €4.64 per day up to a maximum of 15), the Estación Sur and Conde de Casal bus stations, and lockers at Atocha (open 6.30am–10.20pm) and Chamartín (open 7am–11.30pm) train stations.

Opening hours Spain in general, and Madrid in particular, operate on a dif-

ferent clock to much of Europe. Smaller shops generally open 10am–2pm and 5–8pm Mon to Fri, but only open in the mornings on Sat Department stores and chains tend not to close for lunch, open all day Sat, and larger ones open on the first Sun of the month too (except in Aug). Restaurants generally serve from 1.30 to 4pm and 8.30pm to midnight, with many closing for a rest day on Mon. Bars stay open till the early hours – usually around 2am – while clubs and discobares can open until around 5am, depending on the licence they hold.

Pharmacies Farmacias are distinguished by a green cross and can be found across the city. Each district has a pharmacy staying open through the night – for details check the notice on the door of your nearest one or call ☎098 (Spanish only).

Police If you've had something stolen call ☎902 112 102 (English spoken) or head to one of the following centrally located police stations (comisarías) to report the crime: c/Luna 29 (☎915 211 236; Metro Callao), c/Huertas 76–78 (☎913 221 027; Metro Antón Martín) or c/Leganitos 19 (☎915 487 985; Metro Santo Domingo). You will need to fill in an official report (denuncia) for insurance purposes which can be a time-consuming business. In an emergency call ☎112, for the municipal police call ☎091 and for the national police call ☎092.

Post office A centrally located post office can be found in El Corte Inglés, c/Preciados 1 (Metro Sol) and there is another with extended hours at c/Mejía Lequerica 7 (Metro Alonso Martínez). The easiest places to buy stamps (sellos) are the estancos, recognizable by their brown and yellow signs bearing the word Tabacos.

Public holidays The main national holidays when shops and banks close are: Jan 1 (Año Nuevo); Jan 6 (Reyes); Easter Thursday (Jueves Santo); Good Friday (Viernes Santo); May 1 (Fiesta del Trabajo); May 2 (Día de la Comunidad); May 15 (San Isidro); Aug 15 (Virgen de la Paloma); Oct 12 (Día de la Hispanidad); Nov 1 (Todos Los Santos); Nov 9 (Virgen de la Almudena); Dec 6 (Día de la Constitución); Dec 8 (La Inmaculada); Dec 25 (Navidad).

Safety and crime Central Madrid is so densely populated – and so busy at just about every hour of the day and night – that it seems to carry very little "big city" threat. However, that's not to say that crime is not a problem, nor that there aren't any sleazy pockets to be avoided. Tourists in Madrid, as everywhere, are prime targets for **pickpockets** and petty thieves so take care in crowded areas, on buses, in the metro, burger bars and in the Rastro. Be aware also that although the city council is taking some measures to combat the problem, the main routes through Casa de Campo and the Parque del Oeste are still frequented by prostitutes and their clients and are best steered clear of at night. Calle Montera, near Sol, and some of the streets just to the north of Gran Vía are also affected by the problem, and so it is worth taking a little extra care around here.

Smoking Be aware that many Spaniards are heavy smokers and routinely ignore no-smoking signs while the government's attempt to reduce smoking in public places has backfired spectacularly. The *ley de anti-tabaco* gave smaller bars and restaurants the choice to become either smoking or non-smoking with the vast majority voting for the former. Larger establishments have to set aside a non-smoking area, but non-smoking bars and restaurants remain a rarity. Terrace bars are often the best option if you are with children and want a smoke-free zone.

Swimming pools and aquaparks The Piscina Canal Isabel II, Avda de Filipinas 54 (daily 10am–8.30pm; Metro Ríos Rosas), is a large and well-maintained outdoor swimming pool, and the best central option. Alternatively, try the open-air *piscina* in the Casa de Campo (daily 10am–8.30pm; Metro El Lago). Both pools have café/bars attached. The rooftop pool of the *Hotel Emperador* (see p.170) on Gran Vía offers fantastic views across the city but costs a fortune for non-residents (June–Sept Mon–Thurs €25, Fri–Sun €35). There are also a number of aquaparks around the city, the closest being Aquamadrid, 16km out on the N-II Barcelona road (Bus Continental Auto #281, #282, #282, or #385 from Avda de América). Outside May–Sept most outdoor pools are closed.

Telephones International calls can be made from any phone box or *locutorio* (call centre). The main Telefónica office at Gran Vía 30 has ranks of phones and is open until midnight. Phones accept either coins or phonecards that cost €5, €10, €15 and €20 from post offices or *estancos*. Calling Madrid from abroad, dial your international access code, then 34, followed by the subscriber's number which will nearly always start with 91. Mobile phone users from the UK should be able to use their phones in Spain – check with your service provider before leaving about costs. Most American cellphones do not work with the Spanish mobile network.

Theatre As befits the nation's capital, Madrid has a vibrant theatre scene which, if you speak the language, is well worth sampling. You can catch anything from Lope de Vega to contemporary and experimental productions, and there is a particularly good range on offer during the annual *Festival de Otoño* which runs from Septr to Nov. For information on current productions, check the listings sources on p.176.

Ticket agencies For theatre and concert tickets try: ⊛www.entradas.com, ☎902 221 622; Caixa de Catalunya/Tele Entrada ☎902 101 212, ⊛www.telentrada.com; Caja de Madrid ☎902 488 488; El Corte Inglés ☎902 400 222, ⊛www.elcorteingles.es; FNAC ☎915 956 100; TickTackTicket ☎902 150 02, ⊛www.ticktackticket.com; and Servi-Caixa ☎902 332 211, ⊛www.servicaixa.com. Localidades Galicia, Plaza del Carmen 1, ☎915 312 732, ⊛www.eol.es/lgalicia sells ticket for football matches, bullfights, theatres and concerts.

Time Madrid is one hour ahead of Greenwich Mean Time during winter and two hours ahead from March to Oct. Clocks go forward in late March and back an hour in late Oct.

Tipping Tipping is not as important in Spain as it is, say, in the United States. Adding around five to ten percent to a restaurant bill is perfectly acceptable (more if the service was exceptional), while in bars and taxis, rounding up to the nearest euro is the norm.

Travel agents Viájes Zeppelin Plaza Santo Domingo 2 (☎915 477 904, ⊛www.v-zeppelin.es; Metro Santo Domingo), are English-speaking and very efficient. The popular high-street agencies Halcón Viajes (C/Goya 23) and Viajes Marsans (Gran Vía 63) have other branches across the city and are a good place to find hotel vouchers. Many other travel agents are concentrated on and around Gran Vía & c/Princesa.

Fly Less – Stay Longer

Rough Guides believes in the good that travel does, but we are deeply aware of the impact of fuel emissions on climate change. We recommend taking fewer trips and staying for longer. If you can avoid travelling by air please use an alternative, especially for journeys of under 1000km/600 miles. And always offset your travel at ⊛www.roughguides.com/climatechange.

Chronology

Chronology

800s ▶ Muslims establish a defensive outpost on the escarpment above the River Manzanares. It becomes known as "mayrit" – the place of many springs – successively modified to Magerit and then Madrid.

1086 ▶ Madrid taken by the Christians under Alfonso VI, but it remains a relatively insignificant backwater.

1561 ▶ Felipe II chooses Madrid as a permanent home for the court because of its position in the centre of the recently unified Spain. The population surges with the arrival of the royal entourage and there is a boom in the building industry.

1700–1746 ▶ With the emergence of the Bourbon dynasty under Felipe V, a touch of French style, including the sumptuous Palacio Real, is introduced into the capital.

1759–88 ▶ Carlos III tries to make the city into a home worthy of the monarchy. Streets are cleaned up, sewers and street lighting installed, and work begins on the Museo del Prado.

1795–1808 ▶ Spain falls under the influence of Napoleonic France, with their troops entering the capital in 1808. The heavily out-gunned Madrileños are defeated in a rising on May 2 and Napoleon installs his brother Joseph on the throne.

1812–14 ▶ The French are removed by a combined Spanish and British army and the monarchy makes a return under the reactionary Fernando VII.

1833–1875 ▶ Spanish society is riven with divisions which explode into a series of conflicts known as the Carlist Wars and lead to chronic political instability, including a brief period as a republic.

1875–1900 ▶ Madrid undergoes significant social changes prompted by a rapid growth in population and the emergence of a working class. The socialist party, the PSOE, is founded in the city in 1879.

1923–1931 ▶ A hard-line military regime under Miguel Primo de Rivera takes control, with King Alfonso XIII relegated to the background. The king eventually decides to abdicate in 1931 and the Second Republic is ushered in.

1936–39 ▶ The Right grows increasingly restless and a group of army generals organize an uprising in July 1936 which ignites the Spanish Civil War. Madrid resists and becomes a Republican stronghold.

1939 ▶ Franco and his victorious Nationalists enter the city. Mass reprisals take place and Franco installs himself in the country residence of El Pardo.

1939–1953 ▶ Spain endures yet more suffering during the post-war years until a turnaround in American policy rehabilitates Franco, as they search for anti-Communist Cold War allies.

1970s ▶ Franco eventually dies in November 1975. He is succeeded by King Juan Carlos who presides over the transition to democracy.

1981 ▶ In a last-gasp attempt to re-establish itself, the military under Colonel Tejero storms the parliament in Madrid, but a lack of support from the king and army cause its collapse. The Socialists led by Felipe González win the 1982 elections.

1980s ▶ Freedom from the shackles of dictatorship and the release of long-pent-up creative forces help create *La Movida* as Madrid becomes the place to be.

1990s ▶ The Socialists become increasingly discredited as they are engulfed in a web of scandal and corruption, losing control of Madrid in 1991 and the country in 1996 to the conservative Partido Popular (PP).

2004 ▶ The March 11th bombings carried out by Muslim extremists at Atocha train station kill 191 and injure close to 2000. The Socialists return to power in the general elections which follow, although the PP remain firmly in control of the local government.

Language

de nada	not at all/you're welcome
¿Habla (usted) inglés?	Do you speak english?
(no) hablo español	I (don't) speak Spanish
Me llamo ...	My name is...
¿Cómo se llama usted?	What's your name?
Soy inglés(a)/ escocés(a)/ galés(a)/ australiano(a)/ canadiense americano(a)/ irlandés(a)/ neocelandés(a)	I am English/ Scottish/Welsh/ Australian/ Canadian/ American/ Irish/ a New Zealander

Hotels, transport and directions

Quiero	I want
Quisiera	I'd like
¿Sabe....?	Do you know…?
No sé	I don't know
(¿)hay(?)	there is (is there)?
Deme (uno así)	Give me (one like that)
¿Tiene...?	Do you have…?
la hora una habitación con dos camas/cama matrimonial	the time a room with two beds/ double bed
con ducha/baño	with shower/bath
es para una persona	it's for one person
para una noche	for one night
para una semana	for one week
¿por dónde se va a....?	how do I get to…?
izquierda, derecha, todo recto	left, right, straight on
¿Dónde está la estación de autobuses/la oficina de correos/ el baño?	Where is the bus station/post office/toilet?
¿Cómo se llama ésto en español?	What´s this in spanish?
¿De dónde sale el autobús para...?	Where does the bus to... leave from?
quisiera un billete (de ida y vuelta) para...	I'd like a (return) ticket to...
¿a qué hora sale?	What time does it leave?

Money

¿Cuánto es?	How much?
Me gustaría cambiar dinero	I would like to change some money
cajero automático	ATM cash machine
La Oficina de cambio	Foreign exchange bureau
Tarjeta de crédito	Credit card
Cheques de viaje	Travellers' cheques

Numbers/days/months/seasons

un/uno/una	1
dos	2
tres	3
cuatro	4
cinco	5
seis	6
siete	7
ocho	8
nueve	9
diez	10
once	11
doce	12
trece	13
catorce	14
quince	15
diez y seis	16
diez y siete	17
veinte	20
veintiuno	21
treinta	30
cuarenta	40
cincuenta	50
sesenta	60
setenta	70
ochenta	80
noventa	90
cien(to)	100
ciento uno	101
doscientos	200
quinientos	500
mil	1000
lunes	Monday
martes	Tuesday
miércoles	Wednesday
jueves	Thursday
viernes	Friday
sábado	Saturday
domingo	Sunday
hoy	today
ayer	yesterday
mañana	tomorrow

enero	January
febrero	February
marzo	March
abril	April
mayo	May
junio	June
julio	July
agosto	August
septiembre	September
octubre	October
noviembre	November
diciembre	December
primavera	Spring
verano	Summer
otoño	Autumn
invierno	Winter

Food and drink

aceitunas	olives
agua	water
ahumados	smoked fish
al ajillo	with olive oil and garlic
a la marinera	seafood cooked with garlic, onions and white wine
a la parilla	charcoal-grilled
a la plancha	grilled on a hot plate
a la romana	fried in batter
albóndigas	meatballs
almejas	clams
anchoas	anchovies
anís	aniseed liqueur
arroz	rice
asado	roast
bacalao	cod
berenjena	aubergine/eggplant
bocadillo	french-loaf sandwich
boquerones	small, anchovy-like fish, usually served in vinegar
café (con leche)	(white) coffee
calamares	squid
callos	tripe
cangrejo	crab
caracoles	snails
carta	menu
cebolla	onion
cena	supper
cerveza	beer
champiñones	mushrooms
chorizo	spicy sausage
cochinillo	roast suckling pig
cocido	meat and chickpea stew
comida	food/lunch
conejo	rabbit
croquetas	croquettes, usually with bits of ham in
cuchara	spoon
cuchillo	knife
desayuno	breakfast
empanada	slices of fish/meat pie
ensalada	salad
ensaladilla	Russian salad (diced vegetables in mayonnaise, often with tuna)
fresa	strawberry
gambas	prawns
higado	liver
huevos (revueltos/fritos)	(scrambled/fried) eggs
jamón serrano	cured ham
jamón de york	regular ham
langostinos	langoustines
lechuga	lettuce
manzana	apple
mejillones	mussels
menú (del día)	daily set-lunch
menú de degustación	set menu offering a taste of several house specialities
morcilla	black pudding
naranja	orange
ostras	oysters
pan	bread
patatas alioli	potatoes in garlic mayonnaise
patatas bravas	fried potatoes in a spicy tomato sauce
pimientos	peppers
pimientos de padrón	small peppers, with the odd hot one thrown in
piña	pineapple
pinchos/pintxos	a small bite-sized tapa
pisto	assortment of cooked vegetables, similar to ratatouille

For more information go to www.roughguides.com

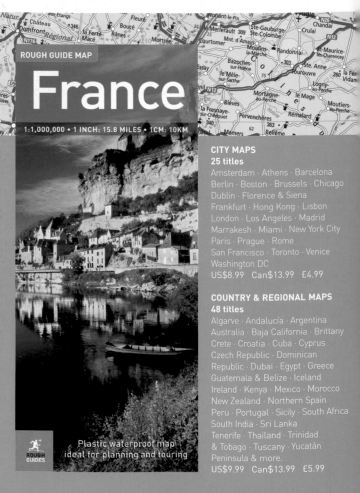

small print & Index

A Rough Guide to Rough Guides

In 1981, Mark Ellingham, a recent graduate in English from Bristol University, was travelling in Greece on a tiny budget and couldn't find the right guidebook. With a group of friends he wrote his own guide, combining a contemporary, journalistic style with a practical approach to travellers' needs. That first Rough Guide was a student scheme that became a publishing phenomenon. Today, Rough Guides include recommendations from shoestring to luxury and cover hundreds of destinations around the globe, including almost every country in the Americas and Europe, more than half of Africa and most of Asia and Australasia. Millions of readers relish Rough Guides' wit and inquisitiveness as much as their enthusiastic, critical approach and value-for-money ethos. The guides' ever-growing team of authors and photographers is spread all over the world.

In the early 1990s, Rough Guides branched out of travel, with the publication of Rough Guides to World Music, Classical Music and the Internet. All three have become benchmark titles in their fields, spearheading the publication of a range of more than 350 titles under the Rough Guide name, including phrasebooks, waterproof maps, music guides from Opera to Heavy Metal, reference works as diverse as Conspiracy Theories and Shakespeare, and popular culture books from iPods to Poker. Rough Guides also produce a series of more than 120 World Music CDs in partnership with World Music Network.

Visit www.roughguides.com to see our latest publications.

Rough Guide travel images are available for commercial licensing at www.roughguidespictures.com

Publishing information

This 2nd edition published March 2008 by
Rough Guides Ltd, 80 Strand, London WC2R 0RL.
345 Hudson St, 4th Floor, New York, NY 10014,
USA.

Distributed by the Penguin Group
Penguin Books Ltd, 80 Strand, London WC2R 0RL
Penguin Group (USA), 375 Hudson Street, NY
10014, USA
14 Local Shopping Centre, Panchsheel Park, New
Delhi 110017, India
Penguin Group (Australia), 250 Camberwell Road,
Camberwell, Victoria 3124, Australia
Penguin Group (Canada), 10 Alcorn Avenue,
Toronto, ON M4V 1E4, Canada
Penguin Group (NZ), 67 Apollo Drive, Mairangi Bay,
Auckland 1310, New Zealand
Typeset in Bembo and Helvetica to an original
design by Henry Iles.

Cover concept by Peter Dyer.

Printed and bound in China

© Simon Baskett 2007

No part of this book may be reproduced in any form
without permission from the publisher except for
the quotation of brief passages in reviews.
208pp includes index

A catalogue record for this book is available from
the British Library

ISBN 978-1-85828-284-8

Help us update

We've gone to a lot of effort to ensure that the first edition of Madrid DIRECTIONS is accurate and up-to-date. However, things change – places get "discovered", opening hours are notoriously fickle, restaurants and rooms raise prices or lower standards. If you feel we've got it wrong or left something out, we'd like to know, and if you can remember the address, the price, the phone number, so much the better.

Please send your comments with the subject line "Madrid DIRECTIONS Update" to ⑥mail@roughguides.com. We'll credit all contributions and send a copy of the next edition (or any other Rough Guide if you prefer) for the very best emails.

Have your questions answered and tell others about your trip at ⑩community.roughguides.com

Rough Guide credits

Text editor: Nikki Birrell
Layout: Ajay Verma
Photography: Tim Draper
Cartography: Jasbir Sandhu

Picture editor: Sarah Cummins
Proofreader: Helen Castell
Production: Rebecca Short
Cover design: Chloë Roberts

SMALL PRINT

The author

Simon Baskett is a writer and journalist who lives and works in Madrid with his wife Trini, and children Patrick and Laura. He's a long-suffering Atlético Madrid fan, and had not given up hope that they might do "the double" again. His ambition is to win El Gordo (the huge Christmas lottery) and retire to a local bar. Simon is also the author of the Rough Guide to Madrid and a co-author of the Rough Guide to Spain.

Acknowledgements

Special thanks to Trini once again for all her hard work and patience, and to Patrick and Laura for just being themselves. Thanks too go to Nikki and all those who gave recommendations or advice for this book.

202

Places
p.52 Plaza de la Villa © Sergio Delle Vedove/Alamy
Palacio Real and Ópera
p.68 Joy Eslava © Imagebroker/Alamy
p.92 Two Old Men Eating, one of the 'Black
Paintings', 1819–23 (oil on canvas) by Goya y
Lucientes, Francisco Jose de (1746–1828) ©
Prado, Madrid, Spain/ Giraudon/ The Bridgeman
Art Library
p.103 Real Fabrica de Tapices © The Royal Tapestry Factory
p.122 Under the Parasol, Zarauz, 1910 by Sorolla
y Bastida, Joaquin (1863–1923) © Museo
Sorolla, Madrid, Spain/ Index/ The Bridgeman
Art Library
p.121 Dama de Elche © Archivo Iconografico,
S.A./Corbis
p.133 Costumes © Museo del Traje
p.144 Jardin del Principe © Kevin George/Alamy
Toledo
p.151 The Burial of Count Orgaz, from a legend
of 1323, detail of a young page, St Etienne,
the Count and St Augustine, 1586–88 (oil on
canvas) (detail of 44240) by Greco, El (Domenico
Theotocopuli) (1541–1614) ©Toledo, S.Tome,
Spain/ The Bridgeman Art Library

Index

Maps are marked in colour